STATE OF THE NATION
Contemporary Zimbabwean Poetry

THE
CONVERSATION
PAPERPRESS

First published 2009 by
THE CONVERSATION PAPERPRESS
Upper Roundell, Park Road, Faversham, Kent ME13 8ES, UK.
www.conversationpoetry.co.uk

ISBN 978-0-9563137-0-6

All rights reserved.

Compilation Copyright © The Conversation Paperpress 2009

© The copyright for all contributions remains that of the author.

This book is sold subject to the condition that it shall not,
by way of trade or otherwise, be lent, re-sold, hired out,
or otherwise circulated without the publisher's prior consent
in any form of binding or cover other than that in which
it is published and without a similar condition including this
condition being imposed on the subsequent purchaser.

Printed and bound in the UK by
Lightning Source, Milton Keynes.

Cover Painting: 'City Blues' by Fisani Nkomo (fisanink@gmail.com)

For Noah and Roseline Mushakawanhu
my beloved parents

and to the future
Tinotenda, Taina & Tawanda Cole

Preface

This anthology comes at a time when Zimbabwe's social and political situation is at the forefront of the mainstream news media's coverage in the UK and elsewhere; at a time when Robert Mugabe still speaks of Britain, first and foremost, in the language of colonialism. We can debate the realities and rhetoric of an antagonistic relationship between the two countries, our interlocked histories, or the nature of consequence. But through the words in the essays and poetry of this book, Zimbabwe's poets tell their own stories: of personal experience, of how the passing of one generation into another is felt and understood.

We have been fortunate enough to collect some of the most important names in Zimbabwean poetry, together with many of the most talented younger poets, in an anthology for the first time in over twenty years. This would not have been possible if not for the hard work and ambition of Tinashe Mushakavanhu, whose original suggestion to me of a special issue of *Conversation Poetry Quarterly* soon spiralled, becoming the book that you hold in your hand. Indeed, The Conversation Paperpress owes its conception to a few dedicated individuals such as Tinashe, who believe in bringing some of the world's rarely heard voices to the pages of European and American poetry.

Zimbabwean poetry has held on to a sense of social history in a way that the poetry of other nations has not: the personal contrasted against a wider backdrop, giving the poems in this collection a clear identity – a series of verses unique to Zimbabwe; where even those poets who have lived away from the country write with a voice that could come from nowhere else.

David Nettleingham

Contents

An Introductory Perspective by Tinashe Mushakavanhu   xiii

Julius Chingono
    A Silhouette   1
    As I Go   2
    My Uniform   3
    The Cult   5
    Zhin-Zhan   6

John Eppel
Essay: Writing in Times of Crisis   8
    Sonnet with One Unstated Line   9
    Cewale   12
    An Awkward Gait   13
    Pungwe [Matobo 1984]   14
    Songbirds   15
    Hillside Road in August   16

Charles Mungoshi
    A Kind of Drought   17
    Nehanda   19
    Unemployed in the Beer Garden   20
    Prayer   22
    The Man Who Ran Away from Pain   23

Dambudzo Marechera
    For Bettina, Tuesday Prologue   24
    Shock: For Bettina   25
    To Bettina, with Angry Tenderness   26

Chenjerai Hove
    Nights with Ghosts   27
    Identity   31
    Embraces in the Rubble   32
    Counting the Nights   33
    Tyrant   35
    The Little Sister   36

Amanda Hammar
Essay: Poetry's Pulse   37
    A Man is Dying for a Piece of Bread   40
    Carla at the Miramar   41
    Zimbabwe Lost   42
    Abandoned   43
    Exiles   44

Kristina Rungano
    Londoners   45
    A World Without Terror   46
    Oh Ye Righteous Men of Babylon   47
    The Sound of Voices   48
    Alien Somebody   49

Jennifer Armstrong
Essay: Let us Examine our Grotesques!   50
    (i)   53
    (ii)   54
    (iii)   55
    (iv)   56
    (v)   57

Nhamo Mhiripiri/J. Tsitsi Mutiti
Essay: Coupling in Words   58

Nhamo Mhiripiri
    Interregnum: the short sleeve or long sleeve choice   62
    When You Meet my Countrymen   63
    In African Gulags   64

J. Tsitsi Mutiti
    Lean Thinking   65
    To Give and Not to Count the Cost   67

Emmanuel Sigauke
Essay: The Origins of my Poetic Journey   70
    A House for Mother   73
    The Village Motto   74
    Bulawayo and Oslo   75
    Gonera Bees   77
    Smitten with Art   78

Christopher Mlalazi
Essay: The Timelessness of Poetry   79
    A Soundless Song   81
    Where Will They Be on Xmas Day?   82
    The Worker's Flag   83
    When Will the Serpent Shed Its Skin?   84
    They Are Coming   85

Josephine Muganiwa
    Nothing for Free   86
    Senior Pastor's Conference   87

Ignatius Mabasa
Essay: The Language I Cry In   88
    Swings and See-saws   92
    Cavities   93
    Concrete and Plastic   94
    Defiance   95
    Poetry   96

Phillip Zhuwao
    ...and love wept   97
    When Thought Remains   98
    Mayakovsky   99
    The Jar of Chrysanthemums   100
    Hush Hush (Harsh) my Love   101

Tinashe Muchuri
    Fifteen Minutes Drive   103
    Mother's Prayer   104
    Running Away Men   105
    Guest of Honour   106
    A Soldier's Confession   107

Ruzvidzo Mupfudza
Essay: Poetry Woos . . . 108
    Quest . . . 110
    A Binge at the Crossroads . . . 111
    Zimlife . . . 112
    Out of Which the Mafia is Hewn . . . 113
    Songs of Bones . . . 115

Zvisinei Sandi
    Is God a Woman? . . . 116
    Exhortation . . . 117

Rumbi Katedza
    An Open Letter . . . 118
    Last Dollar . . . 120

Masimba Biriwasha
    Once upon a Bloody Journey . . . 122
    Wood . . . 123

Togara Muzanenhamo
    The Chronicles . . . 124
    At Measure . . . 126
    A Killing . . . 127
    Buying Out the Dead . . . 128
    Amnesia . . . 130

Batsirai Chigama
    Alien . . . 131
    Poems in an Envelope . . . 132

Beaven Tapureta
    Walking 'n Talking . . . 133
    Worker's Day . . . 134

Cosmas Mairosi
    The Lord is my Shepherd . . . 136
    Amai Chido . . . 138
    Still the Same Peasants . . . 139
    Visions . . . 140
    Freedom . . . 141

NoViolet Bulawayo
    Diaspora   142
    Independence   143
    Balance   144
    Darfur   145
    Souvenir   146

Emmanuel Sairosi
    Soon the Truth Becomes Apparent   147

Kudzai Ndanga
    Songs of Truth   148
    I am Not my Mother's Daughter   149

Tinashe Mushakavanhu
    Essay: Writing from the Offside Position   150
    Entrepreneurship   150
    Tomorrow is Long Coming   152
    The Distorted Looking Glass   153
    In the House of Exile   154
    Crossing the Line   155

Michael Tsingo
    Sovereignty   156

Abel Dzobo
    City Blues   157
    The ZIFA Chairman   158

Notes on Contributors   159

Acknowledgements   164

Selected Bibliography   166

An Introductory Perspective

The genesis of this anthology is the story of my coming of age. In an autographed copy of *Hakurarwi* presented to me for my twenty-first birthday, Chirikure Chirikure wrote: 'Once a poet, forever a poet.' In the morning of my youth, I drifted to Wales to study for a Masters in Creative Writing under the mentorship of the gifted poet, Menna Elfyn, and I was to become the first African to receive the qualification at Trinity College, Carmarthen, now Trinity University College. There, I was the only one like me. There, I felt lost.

More importantly, it was there that the idea of a new anthology of Zimbabwean poetry was born in my homesickness - though it suffered a still-birth. Passion dried so far from the centre. I was out of touch with the goings-on of the motherland. Then my study permit ran out. Instead of disappearing and surviving illegally as an underpaid general BBC (British Bottom Cleaner), I returned home to retain my sanity, to reconnect with my centre, to gain perspective, to seek love and be loved. Once home, everywhere I turned a poem was screaming. Home was still an ancient Queuetopia, where everyone spent long hours in line for everything. Home was the street-level realpolitik that confronted us awake and in dreams. Home was a conference room for the politicos to hold hands with rehearsed camera smiles promising dis-unity. I sought the poets.

For a while, the working title of this book was *Our Poets Speak* because the original concept was to create a kind of sequel to Kadhani and Zimunya's invaluable bible of Zimbabwean verse *And Now the Poets Speak* published in 1982 a year before my birth, because even though Zimbabwean poets had the words to speak the mind of their nation, they were unusually quiet. Then as I read the poems again and again, they suggested a better title, *State of the Nation*, as all the poets represented in the collection give a feeling of the vast and varied canvas that is Zimbabwe, and there is a strong desire in each of them to speak in turn about their country.

***

Publishers in Zimbabwe have certainly failed poetry. Without the imaginative understanding that the poet supplies our culture, literature is in danger of remaining a dull nationalist façade. If no new poets arise to create afresh the associations by which our society can understand itself, we are in danger of carving ourselves a place only in the past. In poetry, the distinction between truth and propaganda is of paramount importance because, as Matthew Arnold once said, 'it is in poetry as a criticism of life and under the conditions fixed for such a criticism by the laws of poetic truth and poetic beauty that the spirit of a country can be preserved for eternity.' (*Matthew Arnold: Selected Prose*)

Publishers in Zimbabwe have been turning to the short story as an alternative 'economic genre' and poetry has been largely ignored apparently for its non-commercial value. More than a dozen short story anthologies have been published since 2000. The greater attention given to Zimbabwean fiction in academic circles in recent years too seems more a reflection upon the critics than upon the continued vigour and invention of the poets. Zimbabwe's turbulent and often tragic progress has not passed unchronicled in poetry.

While young poets can sigh, 'It's the publishers, damn it!' The publishers can simply turn and say, but these 'wannabe' poets lack in quality and style. They lack the understanding and discipline of poetry. They do not read poetry. The best education for any poet is to read other poets. And as my former boss and mentor Irene Staunton used to say to me, experience life first before you think you have something important to say to the world. She was right. What makes us think we have something to say? What makes us think we are versifiers?

Our nation may have verse with smooth rhymes as witnessed by the blossoming and populist *House of Hunger Poetry Slam* and yet may have no real poetry at all. Here is poetry trying to express itself but consumed in too much anger. Anger begets anger. Poetry is emotion controlled. Poetry is message syrupped in language and not a forced political rhetoric. Political or social change always requires an interior swerve away from anger towards a self-disciplined autonomy of spirit.

What the surge of poetic outburst at the Book Cafe presents us with, is Zimbabwe's present psychology and shifting mood swings. It is the temperature of a disillusioned generation, boiling. This is a poetry thirsty for happier conditions of moral and political optimism; it is the voice of a generation crying out loud, 'we have suffered alright but we also want things to be okay.' This poetry is the tempest tearing apart the cloth of old politics that shadows our sense of nationhood. In Zimbabwe, as in Sudan or anywhere else, life may be wretched but it is through poetry that brave spirits leap to respond.

But again, poetry does not necessarily require politics. Politics is about shouting other people down and getting your own way. Good poetry says that politics is all round us. It is sugar queues, it is power outages, it is puddles of sewage in Mbare or Senga, it is the consequences of a convenient creature dubbed the Government of National Unity. The liberating act every poet can perform is to present ideas and imagine alternative realities. I have a conviction that poetry holds, as in a mirror, the climate and scenery of the human soul in its right proportions.

The premise has been that if one has suffered then the statement of one's suffering must be or is poetry. That is wrong. Even Dambudzo Marechera, the darling of young poets across Zimbabwe, knew that the extent to which one has suffered through political oppression is not necessarily the substance of a poem. One has to use certain techniques, certain concentrated, even visionary apprehensions of reality in order to convince the world that suffering is unique and meaningful.

Of course, it does not matter how tough we are, suffering always leaves a scar. It follows us home, it changes our lives. Suffering messes everybody up, but maybe that is the point – all the pain, the fear, the crap. Maybe going through all that is what keeps us moving forward, what pushes us. Maybe we have to get a little messed up before we step.

***

This collection is not produced as a commodity but as part of a long conversation between the present and the past. Zimbabwean poets have always understood that we need an art of our own, to remind us of our history, of what we might be and to show us our true faces – all of them, including the unacceptable, and to speak of what has been muffled in silence. The poets remind us that sometimes the most important history is not what was, but the history that we are making today. Without this history our lives amount to nothing. History is what shapes us, guides us – our history is what defines us.

The background of this poetry is the obscene political situation that developed in Zimbabwe at the turn of the millennium – state violence, spiralling inflation, the high and mighty rise of the guilt-ridden benzocrat, the squalor, the looming and insidious presence of the Problem no one dares mention in public. The poetry whether political or not, is all intensely Zimbabwean and comes out of its landscapes and mindscapes.

In fact, the need to respond to the conditions in Zimbabwean society is in a way allied to the craft of poetry. 'Political' poetry can easily grind down to mere rhetoric and jargon, to become one-dimensional, simplistic, vituperative, but what is often forgotten is that the engagement with 'politics' can force the poets to stretch the resources of language in order to properly confront the monster squeezing the life-blood from their country's bodypolitic.

What I find striking is that most Zimbabwean poets are not so much interested in poetry as an 'artistic genre' but in poetry as a 'medium' to communicate a message. In other words, Zimbabwe is a country of message poets because most of the poetry derives its strength from the force of the message and the message becomes the poem. Perhaps this is what Seamus Heaney meant when he said, 'technique involves not only a poets way with words, his management of metre, rhythm and verbal texture; it involves a definition of his stance towards life, a definition of his own reality.' (*Finders and Keepers*)

The poetry is unmistakably Zimbabwean; its ability to capture and explain the burning questions of the day – issues that are more often than not camouflaged in obtuse state bureaucratese and political rhetoric. Dissonant and unpredictable daily events demand a constant footwork of the imagination, a kind of perpetual translation that a majority of the poets exhibit. There is also the 'expatriate nostalgia' in some of the poems composed from the distance of the Diaspora, verse with a blend of melancholy, memory and fantasy - an enduring feature of exilic sensibility and the crucible of much of this exile poetry. Hence, Zimbabwean poetry is a poetry which is not homogenous but reflects all the different and disparate feelings, experiences and ideas of Zimbabwe.

For a long time, I have longed to read poetry about, and written with, a view to reflect on what Henry Olonga melodiously describes as 'Our Zimbabwe.' A poetry that reflects on the spirit of this country's people through words that survive and vibrate as strongly as that spirit. This is that poetry.

Tinashe Mushakavanhu
Canterbury, August 2009

Julius Chingono

A SILHOUETTE

His eyes are see-through.
Through them I see
a yawning empty bread bin
a fridge stands
astounded
by its chilling emptiness
a stove, cold,
sits huddled in a corner
finds nothing to warm up
for mice swept the pantry
before seeking refuge
in refuse pits
in the neighbourhood.
Cockroaches left jackets
on hangers of webs
bills are forming
a small mound
on a formica table.

Yet - whenever I ask
How he is doing
he replies:
'Fine. And you?'

AS I GO

My pot is an old paint container
I do not know
who bought it
I do not know
whose house it decorated
I picked up the empty tin
in Cemetery Lane.
My lamp, a paraffin lamp
is an empty 280ml bottle
labelled 40 per cent alcohol
I picked up the bottle in a trash bin.
My cup
is an old jam tin
I do not know who enjoyed the sweetness
I found the tin
in a storm-water drain.
My plate is a motor car hub-cap cover
I do not know
whose car it belonged to
I found a boy wheeling it, playing with it .
My house is built
from plastic over cardboard
I found the plastic being blown by the wind
It's simple
I pick up my life
as I go.

MY UNIFORM

When the bread bin
is empty
I put on my uniform
my police officer's uniform
medals dangling down my chest
to the rowdy bread queue
to maintain order
to buy bread
without a hassle

When the maize-meal tin
is low
I put on my uniform
my army officer's uniform
with sergeant's gold stars
pinned on my shoulders
to quick step
to the warlike mealie-meal queue
to buy the mealie-meal
without joining the queue

When I run
out of fuel
I wear my colonel's garb
with its conspicuous badges
swinging around me
to ghost walk
to the bumper to bumper fuel queue
to buy the fuel
from behind the queue

When the family says
sugar is spent

I wear my uniform
my constabulary tunic
to march
to the anxiety charged sugar queue
to suppress all dissent
when I jump the queue

When I go window shopping
I wear my uniform
my patrol officer's reflector vest
weighed down by silver service medals
clanking noisily
to gain quick entry and to travel free
on public transport
These times of shortages
require uniformed strategies
and uniforms of convenience.

THE CULT

The poor are satanic
belong to a cult
that wears lingering linen.
Their two legged vehicles
are soundless
when they move in streets
heavy with darkness.

They converge in families
in dimly lit huts
with no windows
to drink *kachasu*
their wine.
They sing silent hymns
to their gods of want
and thereafter find sleep
on potholed floors
in rooms with falling walls.

ZHIN 'ZHAN'

My friend tells of goings on
In countries of this world
Sometimes he is fond
Of telling lies
He says
There is a country
Whose summer comes
With what he calls
Zhin' zhan' rainfall
That does not last
Accompanied by
Zhin' zhan' lightning
Without thunder
In dark clouds
Seeded with zhin' zhan' chemicals

He carries on
With his fibs
That the country has banks
Zhin' zhan' banks
With zhin' zhan' money
That does not last
That buys
Zhin' zhan' goods only
That do not last

I do not believe him
He can be quite funny
He says
Once every five years
Zhin' zhan' elections are held
To elect a zhin' zhan' government

That makes zhin' zhan' laws
That do not last
And are amended at every seating

I do not know
what zhin' zhan' means
But what I know is
My friend has gone
Zhin' zhan'

John Eppel

WRITING IN TIMES OF CRISIS

I grew up in the shadow of the Second World War, my parents' crisis, who grew up in the shadow of the First World War, my grandparents' crisis. I grew up as a member of an oppressive white minority regime, which sowed the seeds of future personal crises of guilt and alienation. I took part, on the wrong side, in the crisis which came to be known as the Second Chimurenga - the war of liberation. The joy of independence was short-lived: crisis after crisis followed as the politics of patronage and cronyism with its concomitant culture of blame began to destroy our economy. The symbolism of our once proud flag has been replaced by the symbolism of *wabenzi*: the Mercedes Benz. Anybody with a sense of history can see that power corrupts, so that today's oppressed will become tomorrow's oppressors. Davids are Goliaths in waiting. The practice of writing - stories, poems, novels - keeps me detached (sniping distance) from this ugly cycle.

I began writing, poems mainly, in my early teens. At that point I had no political awareness; I grew up - a fourth generation settler - in a small, extremely conservative mining community in rural Matabeleland. I wrote about the so-called deep subjects like God, beauty, love and death. Black people, whose land and whose dignity we had usurped, did not occur to me as a subject worthy of iambic treatment. From the late 60s my first poems began to appear in print. I was about 18 years old. I imitated the poets we had been introduced to by our expatriate primary school teachers: Alfred Noyes, Walter De la Mare, John Masefield, Robert Louis Stevenson among others. The emphasis was on prosody.

Echoes of Orsino! When I became politically aware - it happens late or never in a rugby and barbeque culture - I realised that prosody was not appropriate in the colonial context unless I learned to use it ironically, as a tool of self-criticism, a tool to accuse the culture that produced it. So, I don't write sonnets, I write parodies of sonnets. I reject for my less juvenile verse what J.M. Coetzee wrote about Thomas Pringle's: "The familiar trot of iambic tetrameter couplets reassuringly domesticates the foreign content." However, this sometimes backfires. Readers think I write sonnets and odes and sestinas because I am colonial-minded. Similarly my prose satires are frequently misconstrued. Readers conflate me with my characters, especially the grotesque racists.

Now here is a sample of a sonnet parody. It was published in *White Man Crawling*. It's a response to the government's *Operation Murambatsvina*, "clean out the trash", which resulted in instant homelessness for more than 700 000 poor urban Zimbabweans.

SONNET WITH ONE UNSTATED LINE

See the shambling gait of the unemployed,
the vacant stare of the dispossessed;
the plastic bags by breezes bouyed
or, when evening settles, at rest.
Hear the cry of hornbills lost in yards
of rubble and rags, to split the ears
of those who stand and watch; and the guards
unguarded, hammering, hammering.
Smell the blood and mucous, ashes damp;
breath of birds turned children clamouring,
children clamouring. A tyrant's stamp:
a boot, a fist, a fourteen pounder:
come and witness our city flounder.

The fourteenth line of the sonnet has been appropriated by a very large hammer! I use parody to attack what I consider to be bad behaviour, self-righteousness in particular. My first novel – *D.G.G. Barry's The Great North Road* – the bulk of it, was written in 1978, 15 years before it found a publisher, a tiny poetry press in Cape Town called Carrefour. This press, three years before, had published my first book of poems. It had taken 12 years to find a publisher for those. The editor was Douglas Reid Skinner for whom I am still, despite our differences, grateful. None of the Zimbabwean presses would publish me; none of the mainstream South African presses. Influential academics (and editors of anthologies), not only at home but in those countries starched with political correctness like post-independent South Africa, Germany, Canada, and England, dismissed me as morally questionable or simply ignored me. Until fairly recently, my name did not appear in the bibliography of Zimbabwean authors.

Of my pre-independence contemporaries and the independence generation, black writers like Charles Mungoshi, Musaemura Zimunya, Chenjerai Hove, the late Yvonne Vera, Tsitsi Dangaremga, Shimmer Chinodya, Cont Mhlanga, Chirikure Chirikure.... only one has sincerely accepted me as a fellow writer: the equally ignored Julius Chingono, bless him. The same is true of those white Zimbabwean writers like Peter Godwin, Alexandra Fuller, and Alexander McCall Smith, who have tickled the world's fancy. But the younger generation, they are different; they don't seem to have a problem with my socio-political liabilities. Petina Gappah, Christopher Mlalazi, Brian Chikwava... they talk to me. And guess what? They too are satirists, unafraid to ridicule the regime that thinks nothing of torturing and killing its conceived critics.

Of the many atrocities that have occurred in this country from 1965 and beyond, to an hour ago, the worst by far were the genocidal activities of the North Korean trained Fifth Brigade. No one knows the exact number but it is estimated that about 20,000 innocent people from rural Midlands and Matabeleland were massacred. Ostensibly the role of the Fifth Brigade was to wipe out so-called dissidents, a few hundred ZIPRA soldiers loyal to Joshua Nkomo, who had deserted from the army of "national unity" because, allegedly, they were receiving hostile treatment from the ZANLA soldiers loyal to Robert Mugabe. In reality Joshua Nkomo was closer to the truth when he expressed fears that their role was the imposition of a one-party state in Zimbabwe. The Fifth Brigade was established in the very first year of Independence. President Mugabe called his squad *Gukurahundi*, a Shona expression meaning "the rain which washes away the chaff before the spring rains." Sinister words!

Writers have been afraid to record this dark period of our history, possibly because many of the instigators of *Gukurahundi* are still alive and still very much in power. The one famous writer who did have a go was the late Yvonne Vera. No one can deny her courage in tackling taboo subjects like incest and abortion, but *The Stone Virgins* is abject cowardice. Shona writers with ZANU PF sympathies are still in too much denial to tackle this shameful period, so close to the euphoria of independence from white rule.

I don't only write satire; some of my stories and poems are direct protests, and many of my poems are personal - attempts to do what mainstream poets do - try to transmute private experience into something universal, try to create a world in a grain of sand like, yes, Blake, or Hopkins, or Yeats, or the greatest of them all - Robert Mugabe's and Thabo Mbeki's fellow countryman - Will Shakespeare.

I sometimes feel that the politics of southern Africa, let alone the politics of the rest of the world, is draining me of my satirical energy. Robert Mugabe, Jacob Zuma, King Mswati - who can caricature a caricature? There are richer pickings in the expatriate community and the NGOs that employ them. Ever since Independence in 1980 they have been pouring into Zimbabwe with a mandate to help "actualise" the gains of the revolution. They have a mantra: "black skin good; white skin bad". I'm generalising of course, but like bathos, hyperbole, burlesque, travesty, irony, generalisation is a tool of the satirist. These parasites, many of whom can't find jobs in their own countries, have their cake and eat it. It's easy to go about barefoot when you have twenty pairs of shoes in your cupboard back home. They have good intentions, no doubt about that, but they have no idea how destructive these intentions, "actualised", can become, especially once - after one year, two years, a decade - they up sticks and return home or transfer to some other Godforsaken part of the world, which, nevertheless accepts Visa and American Express.

CEWALE

A river runs past girls and boys, and swerves
as if to miss the donkey cart trotting
out of Lupane. That hint of rotting
faces, breasts, backsides...mouldering bones, serves
to remind us of *Gukurahundi*:
early rain that washes away the dust
of harvests, the chaff of narrowing lust.
A figure out of *Spiritus Mundi*,
which more than troubles the collective sight,
a figure of unlimited power,
his balls grenades, his cock a bayonet,
always confident, always in the right,
chuckles as he plucks a bank-side flower
and tucks it coyly in his epaulette.

AN AWKWARD GAIT

Papa, Daddy, Uncle, Dear Old Man:
what is it about dictators that we
coddle them with terms of affection?
The lion will slaughter, and even eat,
cubs of his rivals. No subordinate
stands in the way of the dominant
white-browed sparrow weaver, the ballast
of whose gonads gives him an awkward flight.
Why do we admire Generals, pity
vendors? Why do we revere lions,
laugh at hyaenas? What is it about
the clenched fist, the conical tower, church
steeples, pyramids, codpieces, that we
adore? Now this Autocrat, the ballast
of whose honorary doctorates gives
him: Uncle, Dear Old Man: an awkward gait.

PUNGWE [MATOBO 1984]

Masoja were speaking in Shona, their sticks
were *mopane* - that wood is like iron;
broke all my arms and this leg that can't bend;
yes, fan belts, *umfo*, and kicking with boots;
made us undress and do sex with a goat;
then with our bums; sang: "*Pasi LoNkomo.*"
But first they *khetha* some youngsters, not me,
was my brother, my cousin, my neighbours...
on one side putting three, other side three;
then they give me a pick and a *fotshol*,
say dig, and I dig; on this side one grave,
other side one, not deep, to end of my
thing; yes, naked in front of our mothers,
our sisters; *gebha* as deep as the end
of your thing: *mbolo*. Made them to kneel
by the side of the graves; shooting them dead.
We were dancing and singing, and screaming
with pain; they beat us and kicked us for hours,
umfo; yes, calling us dissidents,
whilest we sang: "*Pambili LoMugabe.*"

SONGBIRDS

She was harbouring a dissident in her womb;
they unseamed her with a bayonet;
it dangled from her umbilicus
like a jolly-jumper.
And the doves sang:
gukura
hundi,
gukura
hundi.
Little children of "traitors",
transformed by heavy blows -
they use branches, batons, iron bars -
to pumpkins about to spill their seeds.
And the hornbills cry:
Vana
ve nyoka
inyoka
wo futi

HILLSIDE ROAD IN AUGUST

This avenue should have been lined with trees
large enough to nest hamerkops, shelter
vervets, resolve the discord of a breeze;
shade road-rage, allay the helter-skelter
of wheelbarrows, bikes, cars, trucks, juggernauts,
stray donkies, bumless boys with attitude,
buxom girls in tackies and mincing shorts…
trees that could claim the public's gratitude.

Instead it's dotted with colonials
too scrawny for children to climb, or snakes
to whisper in. Yet when that blossom spills
its incense on the smouldering grass, takes
to heart a variegated pink, a white
slipper: there comes a moment of delight.

Charles Mungoshi

A KIND OF DROUGHT

In our land
We found a bird
that sings.
A bird
that will tell it all:
We can't trust humans anymore:
>What if –
>What if we send
>What if the one we send
>What if the only one available
is the father of
the mother of
the uncle of
the aunt of the sister of – ?
In our land
We – you – all – are alone.
Everyone you know (or knew) is gone!
Everyone you thought you knew
you don't know anymore.
Only roads.
Only roads don't betray.
(Pot-holed though they may be.)
No, roads don't lie.
They always bring you
or someone like you
to bump into each other
round a corner.
Trees, as well.
Trees.
Only trees.
Yes, trees.
They remain

the same old faithful parents.
You can climb them.
You can hide behind them.
(Or go round and round and round
behind, to the side, or in front of them).
You can chew their leaves for water.
You can chew the roots
to cool the pain in belly or limb
and, there is always, always, the fruit.
And, of course, out of the sun, the shade.
And, finally, you can safely die under a tree.
In our land
the trees can be trusted
and sometimes they hide someone
who feels just like you do
and for a while
there are just the two of you
to frighten the darkness away
if only, only if,
if only you can come to a river.

NEHANDA

There is a school, a hospital, a street,
(Even a brothel, you say?)
Maybe two or more than two
of each of these
in one or more than one town
across the whole nation
of the people's memory
of she
whose name now
is a discarded wheelbarrow
a spent firebrand
a hollow shell
that has seen better days.
Those she inspired (or inspires)
now conspire against her
and look away from her
embarrassed
as they tuck wads of banknotes
(Ill-gotten gains, you say?)
into their soiled briefcases.
For these, too,
her bones were resurrected.

UNEMPLOYED IN THE BEER GARDEN

In silence
the beer mug passes from hand to mouth
from chapped lip to roughed hand
until the mug's empty bottom
reflects the emptiness in our future plump faces.
We begin to put up together a great republic
such as has never been seen before on this earth.
There, the poor (always the poor) are lifted onto
pedestals, they have the pulpits and the podiums
the children (remember the children) sing happy
songs at play
and the air crackles with the laughter
of the toothless aged and the harmless impotent.
The rich?
Abasha!
Down with!
The rich are stripped down
to their bare bones and thrown into dungeons.
They are now the hewers of rock
and the drawers of shit.
(They are baking bricks for the pyramids
with grass)
They will now build those schools
those hospitals
those roads,
which they once promised us.
This time they are going to use
their own bloody hands,
rain, thunder or shine, God!
Raise high the whips, boys!
Yoke them together
let them pull the plough in the maize fields.
Give each a huge hoe

let them shore up the tobacco rows
in the plantations – Lord!
Make them chew their own words!
Make them swallow their own medicine.
Send them into the sewers!
Make them sweat blood sweat and tears –
Make them not even touch the crumbs
from the dog's table.
Let them see unreason!

PRAYER

It would be very convenient now
to kneel down in the gritty sand
and beat my chest
and rend my garments
and cry out: "Why me, O Lord?"
It would be an admirable thing to do
if it weren't for the refrain
running beneath it all:
"Do you see me now, Lord?
Aren't I just wonderful!"
Until, just like the worst
of all the best of us
I, too, am ambushed
before I have made
my last prayer.

THE MAN WHO RAN AWAY FROM PAIN

He ran away from home
where, he thought, all pain
began.
He went to another country
Where he discovered
the pain of leaving home.

Dambudzo Marechera

FOR BETTINA, TUESDAY PROLOGUE

From nightsky's black earth
Rare lilies, like stars,
Flower into life, yours and mine.
Orion, Andromeda, these startling sickles.
Of each our nights, recumbent beyond mere mortal
Rest, are not fixed but pliant to our motion
When courage lip to lip embraces despair.
Do not to the deep sorrow surrender
But ever twine upward to the silver light
Eyes a blast furnace terror to untruth.
Through windowpane I view the wide vistas
Of improbability become possible, hugging each to
Other in heartrending love: no more the one step
That's a giant stride for mankind, but you and I
In fiery leap burning bright become starfruits
Over stony ground.

SHOCK: FOR BETTINA

Like meteorites, through my long
Isolated heart-atmosphere, you
Burst incandescent over my platinum history.
My future in earthquake reeled; my present only on
Seismograph could point to the cataclysm – no
Evidence of you attached to my stone and flesh,
Only nightmarish passions which I can still hear
When you shake your head. Shake it vigorously.
Nuclear tests of underground love!

TO BETTINA, WITH ANGRY TENDERNESS

Great Zimbabwe, Matopos: they to me return
You feverish with visions of mortality:
I dare not hold your fragility tightly
But through anger's gentle kiss remould you
With my intimacy to your former state.
Brief acquaintance, dredged by shared experience,
Is now a harbour for the biggest tankers
Or the human spirit: Mainz, Harare. Maputo,
Cologne, Lusaka: the loneliest breeze
Is part of the astounding cyclone.
Forget ever the pain that teases your eternal sight:
Finite impurities will never dim your tormented inscape!

Chenjerai Hove

NIGHTS WITH GHOSTS

dear samueri, my friend
i will never see you again;
maybe i will.
but i shall not know
until father finds us a new address.
we have none anymore.
we are of no address.

now that i have written this letter,
where do i post it to?
shall i say, samueri,
care of the next rubble
harare?

or shall i say,
samueri,
care of all the filth,
salisbury?

our little street,
you remember?
the one without broken glass,
the one where we urinated freely
behind the small market
and our mother called us names
with the sweet voices of mothers?
our little street, with chickens that belonged to no one
in particular, is no longer there:

i don't know your address,
you don't know my address,
samueri,
i am standing on a broken brick,

the only survivor
of our home.
what are you standing on,
samueri?

you see, samueri,
we don't have guns
or spears
or arrows,
or sticks.
tell me,
samueri,
why police,
they bring guns
hammers
anger
blood in their eyes
to destroy our only home?

even teacher mutawu,
he also has no address.
i saw our school in the fire.
i saw our teacher crying,
carried away by police
with guns and anger.

i will continue writing this letter,
samueri till I know your address
teacher mutawu's address
my father's work address
my little sister's address
my little dog's address
my mother's address
everyone's address,

care of spca
care of filth department
care of order
care of Caledonia camp,
care of tribal trust land
care of the river bank!
care of cockroach camp!
care of maggots
care of crime and grime
care of state house!

samueri,
tell teacher mutawu,
i want to learn to write
so i can erase memories
of our home
in the rubble.

tell teacher mutawu,
we will meet
when i have grown a beard
and drive a car
like the police car
like the soldiers with guns.

samueri,
i send you only
a broken brick
before they break it again
for the second time
the third time
the fourth time.

a broken brick, a broken heart
a broken father, a broken mother.

samueri, stay strong.
samueri,
beware of falling bricks
and guns.

IDENTITY

Far away from home,
The smells,
The sounds,
the madness,
the laughter,
the sorrows
and joys of the
land of my birth,
the songs of the birds
whose names I know,
the sounds of the rivers
whose names
I grew up naming
with rhythm and dance,
the shapes of the hills and mountains,
how they told us
they looked like a man dancing,
a woman smoking a pipe,
a crazy woman dancing to several lovers,
the colours of the sky
as it changes its many tempers
to invoke the voice of thunder and lightning,
all those colours of butterflies and nameless things,
all these will always remind me
that I am part of that geographical
space where I grew up.
It is my traveller's luggage,
in my soul and heart,
while I travel and reach
out to other lands
which might welcome me
with their own voices.

EMBRACES IN THE RUBBLE

This winter
our last embrace,
the one we did not have,
was clouded in whispers.
You, a mere photo,
me, a shadow of disbelief,
We walk on
with outstretched arms,
our souls broken by the sharp winds.

With your feet cold
in the wintry air
you cried for empty nipples.
With my hope cold
in the fiery air
I missed you still.

Child,
where might you be,
in this nightmare?
Where might I be,
in this swamp of despair?

In the rubble,
maybe your heart still stands firm.
In the rubble,
maybe I will pick up some pieces
of the love a bulldozer can't take away.

All we know now,
we are nobody's national plan,
or wordless anthems.

COUNTING THE NIGHTS

Another night
spent without you.
Another echo
in the distance,
far away from my dirty fingers.

I let sunlight
filter
through my numb fingers.
For once,
the silent echoes crush my heart.

No,
this is a dream I did not dream.
Was it your birthday today?
And the wind carried away
the cakes littering my mind?
Was it someone's funeral today?
A funeral with more corpses
than mourners?

Oh, this distant place
they call birthday!
Oh, this intimate place
they call deathday!

All places are faded
in these tremors of bleeding hearts,
you, far away,
me, so frighteningly near myself,
but torn
between nearness and far away.

just take your time,
count the leftover trinkets
in your palms.
Count the lone stars
left gazing at you,
Smile along
hum along
like our little honey-bird.

TYRANT

Why cry
for the wingless spirit bird?
Why cry
for the honey-bird?

The king attends a funeral
and dances with his eyebrows,
his naked words smelling of sand
and gunpowder.

The polluted wind
only smells of lost dreams,
some kinds of amorphous declarations
about blood mixed with dance songs.

Our royal king
smokes a tired cigarette
and eats biscuits with a fork.

He lives in volcanic tempers,
sniffing the wind for armed insurgency
in all locked places.

The king,
he wears necklaces of bullets
his lips stiff with pronouncements.

Tomorrow's funeral
is banned,
the corpse
detained
for further
questioning.

THE LITTLE SISTER

She likes to walk to the local church
and prays Sundays and weekdays.
She likes fresh flowers,
laying them on other people's graves.
She smells the flowers
before kneeling at gravesides.

The little sister, she likes dolls.
Every Saturday she has a new doll
that she likes to bury in the sand.
Then she takes flowers to the doll-grave
early on Sunday morning.

She hums ancient church songs
but does not like to dance.
She sometimes giggles at nothing
without anyone hearing.
The little sister,
she wears her blue dress for all occasions.

Unkind tongues of the street
already dance about a possible funeral.
The little sister,
she will die one of these days,
and no one will attend her funeral.

Amanda Hammar

POETRY'S PULSE

Many years ago, I read a line in an interview with American poet, Tilly Olsen, that had great resonance for me. "I write to survive", she had said. I still identify with that line, but in a sense I now find it insufficient as either an explanation or exploration of why I write, and especially why I write poetry. Writing poetry is about far more than mere survival. It's about living, or trying to live, in an increasingly expansive and connected way.

Poetry calls me out – both writing and reading it. It beckons me to listen more closely to my own beating heart, and to hear its connection to the world's many complex rhythms. And then it asks me to speak from that place of connection – softly or loudly, sadly or joyously, angrily or forgivingly, intimately or more distantly – using the words that are my life-blood.

> I witness the horrors of violence and dislocation that my state and its minions perform in the name of sovereignty and revolution, against those of its citizens deemed 'enemies' or 'dirt'. It is impossible not to write a poem about it.

> I read of a young Zimbabwean man in Cape Town whose aching search for an ordinary life has been tragically curtailed by the crude neglect of political and economic systems that both create and ignore the marginalized. It is impossible not to write a poem about it.

> I cross a street in a Swedish town, and see an old man with a prosthetic leg trip and fall, his leg flying off onto the road. I help him to recover it, watch him replace it, assist him to get up, watch him walk away with grace. This unexpected encounter underscores the shifting border between the false and the real, between shame and dignity. It is impossible not to write a poem about it.

In a first meeting in June 2009 in Uppsala with Zimbabwean poet and literary scholar, Kizito Muchemwa, we talk about what it means to be a Zimbabwean poet. The conversation is charged with questions that float and settle, explicitly and implicitly probing: who can call himself or herself a 'Zimbabwean' poet; does location matter; does exile/proximity make one less or more Zimbabwean; what it is we can or should, or should not, write about, or should that even be a question at all? Afterwards, and perhaps unsurprisingly, I find myself writing a poem that includes these lines:

> We are from the same place
> and not, and anyway somewhere else right now
> asking each other, what is the poetry of home,
> who the legitimate poets of home?
> Is it about being there or being from there,
> having it always speak to you and through you,
> or can we write freely
> of other things and places, beyond the impossible weight
> of our country's soiled history, its fractured urgencies;
> can we write unashamedly
> of seemingly ordinary things: midsummer's eve,
> a son's necessary leaving, the making of a book?

I am both a poet and a Zimbabwean poet (and many other things besides). Zimbabwe is the bones of me. This is not simply a matter of birth, or formal citizenship, though these do count. It is a matter of connection at the deepest levels. It is those earliest warm-toned voices that transformed me from newborn into human; those sensitivities generated by my first encounters of the pain of others' otherness; the earthy, wood-smoked scents, wintered pink-and-gold vlei, dark-skied summer storms, that brought my senses to life. Later, the years spent building a newly independent country with colleagues and friends. And later still, witnessing and mourning and raging together against its 'soiled history, its fractured urgencies'.

And always words. Words that squeezed themselves through my veins, to connect me, eye to eye, skin to skin, breath to breath, pulse to pulse, with the world I inhabited. Perhaps then I should say, Zimbabwe is the poetry of me.

And yet as deep and persistent, if also changing, the connections are to Zimbabwe itself, I can say now – with a sobering sense of liberation that seems necessary for growth not only as an individual, and as a socially responsible and responsive being, but also as a poet – that I am no longer solely defined by my Zimbabwean-ness. While for some, such a condition may seem unremarkable, for me it is both a new sensation and a big and painful admission. But as I grow accustomed to saying it, to feeling it, I realize it isn't about loss or abandonment (in either direction). It is, I think, about finally trusting its presence within me no matter what. No matter where I am or who or what I am. No matter what I experience or feel. No matter what I write about.

A MAN IS DYING FOR A PIECE OF BREAD

for Adonis Musati, Zimbabwean asylum seeker

a man is lying dead
on a busy street
in carefree cape town
the crumbs of excess
elude him

he is far from home
and alone
an ordinary young man
in want of an ordinary life
or just a piece of bread

and so he eats his own shadow
consumes the last twinkle in his eye
swallows handfuls of poisonous hope

his teeth crack biting the pavement
the world passes by
except those who know
the taste of a shadow
and stop to mourn him

CARLA AT THE MIRAMAR

Dry laughter bursts
from her narrow throat
like a stampede of wildebeest
kicking up dust.

She was holding court at the bar.
Behind her the dull-brown Beira sea
a mocking backdrop to the bravado.
Later she sauntered over,
high heels tapping against
the chipped concrete floor,
faded red skirt clinging
to her weightless body.
And tucked into the frayed collar
of her turquoise blouse, a spray
of pink flowers, petals falling
as she walked towards me,
one hand extended, the other fluttering;
a bruised wing.

Our hands meet, strangers' palms
finding an unexpected equivalence.
In the safety of brevity
a bracketed recognition:

(presence   flesh   life   death).

ZIMBABWE LOST

I

What kind of African.
My skin
the colour of colonisation.

II

Rooted baobab-deep.
Orphaned now
by the quarrels of history.

III

Moving
from an ache to an agony
flesh tears from bone
heart from home.

ABANDONED

house
too long abandoned
weeds pushing apart
scarred bricks
beams of weathered wood
exposed like ribs
no longer able to hold in
the soft heartbeat of
home

EXILES

Whenever I make tea,
memories of you surface
like small tricks of proximity;
a temporal sleight of hand.

Years ago in a council flat in Chalk Farm,
we exchanged gifts: mine for the birth of your daughter,
yours Darjeeling tea from the mountains of your birth,
each a marker of origins.

I remember always as I stand pouring boiling water
over leaves darkening at the bottom of the cup,
your affectionate reprimand that day
to let it brew longer, longer than I did then:

your unspoken command
(an unconscious prayer)
to let the leaf know itself fully
in the grace of its sacrifice,

but also your implicit claim
of history as authority:
an instinctive line of defense
against the endless exiles of your present.

Kristina Rungano

LONDONERS

We huddled on street corners
Coughing like hags
Feet suffocating in great big leathers
Rooted in muck and slime
The smoke from our cigarette butts
Escaping into the already scented air
And finding freedom amongst its friends
The unmistakable aroma of urine and un-cleanliness.
Where once our skin had known the softness of youth
Now lay chunks of flesh
Taut and fibrous
Stretching like used twine
As it built a wall against wind and cold
Our noses twitched;
Trembling lips went dry; unsmiling
We looked into each other's eyes where pain lay
Silent and cold;
Someone belched
And released a load of last night's merriment
Last evening we had known bliss in pubs
And in the morning light;
Souls loitering in weary bodies
We held each other close
And looked to the approaching bus
Which we scrambled into
Our jeans scrubbing in the metal railings
Till we found solace in the upper deck
Where herds of cattle might have passed on sand.
We peered through the dust for seats
And there stretched our legs and laughed
For we knew not how death haunted us
Such was the gift of civilisation!

A WORLD WITHOUT TERROR

These are no longer the cruel times of our fathers
Yet
Still we trade their laws for ours
One near sighted lie mocks the other
We are most righteous still
Till they believe what we believe
And
Of all the most painful un-clever things
There is always war
Men throwing bombs in the name of human rights.

No longer some moonstruck wintry spell
Still fills the brink of our being with the totality of our impunity.

Tell me
What is the difference between a tyrant who beats people up
When they question his dream
And members of a G8 who throw bombs
And make their righteous assertion
If you are not with us, you are against.
I feel it sometimes
Why the sound of some ancient Tsunami
Will never penetrate
The walls of human despair
When ours is the better testimony still.

They remain thankless yet.

OH YE RIGHTEOUS MEN OF BABYLON

We've had our white Christmas
And built snow men in the park
We've learnt to call them snow people.
And yet there is not a free man amongst us all.
We still throw bombs
To conceal the treachery of our hearts.
Oh, how I long for the sweet sands of home
And the thunderstorms on Xmastide
We roasted mealie cobs on open fires and watched
The raindrops sing their merry songs
Before we turned round and said our Amen's.

THE SOUND OF VOICES

Now you've known me well
I heard your first tune most
The other got confused in the stickiness of your fingers.
This was when I was socialism
Represented by the people, for the people
I was truth, un-corroded still by the neo-colonialist wand.
I was woe's child, a speaker, a universal king
The man with the loudest laugh
I was a romantic, my mother having crossed
With her father's foe.
I was air, speaking because I had inherited the gift of pain.
I know now who I am
I am a voice which makes no sound.

ALIEN SOMEBODY

I leave behind
The walkways
Smattered still with snow
Each snow flake, cursed within
By the eye behind your window pane.
There was a tree where we could hide
In case the cancerous glow begins to show
They still recall their prayers now
Whilst an alien somebody hides within.

Jennifer Armstrong

LET US EXAMINE OUR GROTESQUES!

Let us suppose that I am a naturally born ironist. If it is possible that I was not actually born that way, it is surely the direct result of bringing myself up in this mode, rather than having had it inculcated into my life by my parents. My idea as to what concerns the pinnacle of education – that is, what expresses the condition of having been well educated – is that one has learned to doubt what one thinks one sees on the basis of the first appearance. I don't think that one can be brought up during the Rhodesian war (the second Chimurenga) and not have had to revise all of one's opinions – one's "first take" of life and its meanings. Perhaps after the second take, a third take and a fourth take are not even enough to satisfy one as the take that is finally the "right take". Not to be completely sure of one's perspectives, but to approach them with a relatively measured certainty is the mark of an educated person's mind. I say it again.

So I want to introduce you to my application of the grotesque. It's not the grotesqueness of a Damudzo Marechera that you will find in my poems. He wants to reveal something with his use of the grotesque – some dimension of the way that torture is generally a hidden mode of societal control. My use of the grotesque has a different purpose. Perhaps you think you see all too clearly what I'm getting at in my poetry? I use the term, "race", so perhaps I am a racist – someone who discriminates between people on the basis of colour? Perhaps I have "issues" concerning gender, and see that there are two genders with one gender distinctly differentiating from the other – since I use language that seems to point things out in this way? Perhaps what I'm saying is all too clear in many ways. I want you to think again.

The language I am using – these ideas – are they really my own? I would like people to consider whether a white girl, a white woman, sits down on any Sunday afternoon and generates out of her imagination, out of the ether that is nothingness, the notion of "race"? Okay! I confess that I didn't do this. I used the word, "race", in my poetry, but there's no way that I generated different races. And, hey, wait a second!

I don't even believe in races! I believe in such a thing as "humanity" – the human race. So I am referring to races, in my poetry. I get caught red-handed. But I don't believe in race. This, then, has now become your puzzle.

It's the puzzle that all of my poetry presents. In actual fact, it is ironic dealing. The subject matter of my writing is not mine, in the sense that it was entirely produced by me. I am just working with the subject matter that was produced by my history - and your history, too, if I am not mistaken. This is the black and white history of Zimbabwe (and Rhodesia), which has given us the remarkable and highly dubious gifts of race and gender. I'm not sure about you, but my perspective on these is a revelation of the grotesque!

I'm like Marechera, in that I want to do something to reorganise your vision, using poetry. Unlike our friend Marechera, I'm not keen so much to reveal to you the hidden dimensions of everyday existence and what you fail to see. Marechera had the sensitivity of a shaman who sees things that few other people do see – as if he looked into the spirit world and saw the dark and estranged aspects of our souls that pulled the mechanisms and pulleys, determining all our fates. His vision was anti-Oedipal and reveals us to ourselves in a way that would allow us to make amends with the past and its historical wrongs. By "anti-Oedipal" I mean that Marechera does not want to bring us under the sway of any new authority or system – whether governed by those of the left or right, white or black. My poetry, on the other hand, is not so kind, and is not (directly at any rate) so conciliatory. My poetry is rather a very Oedipal assault: It says "do you actually see that which you think you see? And if so, how will you cope with your encounter with these apparitions of the grotesque? Once encountered, can we embrace these socially discriminating mechanisms of race and gender? They are our historical creation, but what to do with them? Do we fall back in horror from them, or will we engage in a response of (additional) self-blinding – like Oedipus in fact did, upon finding out that he had inadvertently had sex with his own mother? How we cope with an encounter with the historically manufactured grotesques of gender and race will say a great deal about us in the times to come.

Marechera's approach is, as I said, kinder than mine, in that he reveals, through gently winding narratives, the complex structures of the mind conditioned by a form of society that make us, Zimbabweans, what we are today. My approach is by contrast a throwing down of the metaphorical gauntlet – a challenge to alter one's vision by keeping the eyes open as to the way in which we manufacture social and historical grotesques. Can we still face ourselves – albeit ironically – knowing that we tend to manufacture such grotesques? Can we rise above a naturalistic vision, which sees the development of such creations as natural and nothing to baulk at, to the point where we rise above this terror that's entailed in a realistic encounter with ourselves? At that point, we baulk openly. We will say that we have learned to manage the terror.

And really it is no different from the terror that one feels when one first learns to skydive. You manage the terror then, too, by holding the freezing blade close to your breast: in the desperate pleasure of your own icy resolution.

(i)

In Zimbabwe I lost touch with Marechera's
bleeding heart;
Went to school
white and stiff
My father said;
"It is your fault that us white males lost the war;
because of your genitals and
your demeanour
and the colour of your voice
which reminds me of the feminine."
"His father died in primary school
His father rose again to run the factory"
I'm sure my teacher read it to me
when I was in Form three -
an overlooked and unregarded writer
at that time.
I wonder,
and the school walls and the grass roots kept the ogre at bay
for some time
and we transferred and lost our feet
and ended up eight inches above the sand
in number 3 caravan park;
and it was sordid heat
and three years later, in Australia the sleeping ogre
finally yawned and shook;
the anger at his loss breaking through
the cold tin roof
of his narrow mind.

(ii)

Cultural Destruction
meant that I was now
evil.
One doesn't become evil by any action of one's own;
but by being
left Alone
whilst others are being brought up.
If I cross out my evil
with so many crosses –
Would that help?

(iii)

Feed your children with hostility enough
and you will grow
a little guerilla in your midst.
I didn't want to tell you this
but it is true.
There's no denying
how nature works
when history repeats itself
the first time, Tragedy
and then as Farce.

(**iv**)

Zimbabwe's free
of all the pestilence that
isn't death.
You've got me on that one.
Political Purity
is one thing
that's
INDIFFERENT
to
a little death.

(v)

I don't think
my race
will win
this race
although it might
come second.

Nhamo Mhiripiri/J. Tsitsi Mutiti

COUPLING IN WORDS

We met at the University of Zimbabwe in the early 1990s, fell in love, and attended writing sessions together organised by Chenjerai Hove who was then the Writer-in-Residence at the university. Other young writers who attended these sessions include the late Patrick Machakata (whose ambitious novel *The Far Side of the Moon*, short stories and poetry remain somewhere unpublished), popular praise poet and musician Albert Nyathi, writers and poets Ruzvidzo Mupfudza, Ignatius Mabasa and Memory Chirere. The late rather eccentric student activist Lawrence "Warlord" Chakeredza was also part of this group of literature enthusiasts coming from different academic disciplines. Joyce was then a Metallurgy student in the Faculty of Engineering, and Tariro Mavengere was in Agriculture, with the majority of participants coming from the Faculty of Arts, especially the English Department. Most of these writers cut their teeth in *The Bloom*, a journal of academic writing for students in the English Department that also provided space for short stories and poetry. Our works were first published alongside each other in *The Bloom*. We have since published together in *A Roof To Repair* (College Press 2000), *KOTAZ* (2006), a South African journal for Arts and Culture and *Dreams, Miracles and Jazz: New Adventures in African Writing* (Picador Africa 2008). Joyce uses her second name and maiden name – J. Tsitsi Mutiti - for fictional publications although she uses Mhiripiri for academic publications.

We have always meant to co-author some fictional work together, but this has never actually happened, although we have thought over the same themes and images but have gone on to write distinctly separate individual works. So far we have only co-authored an academic paper on copyright and the Zimbabwe music industry originally derived from Joyce's MBA thesis. Otherwise, we have written individual pieces, addressing each other in a dialogic way, or just reflecting and conversing, so to speak. We have written one or two short stories where we started by discussing a situation. For example, Joyce's story "The Old Woman" which is going to be published in an anthology of African women writing resistance, has its 'sister-story' (if we consider the thematic concerns and the surrounding history of each of the stories) in Nhamo's "Happy New Year". During one crazy mass hysteria period in Zimbabwe when old women were suddenly persecuted in township gossip and urban myth as vampirish witches, we decided to write stories about how old women were generally victims of societal stereotypes and insensitivity.

Yes, we do support each other's creativity, share the same laptop, and edit each other's works. We discuss characters, plots, narrative styles, and the feeling and mood of our individual works. Much as we have different writing styles, we tend to empathise with each other's visions and sensibilities. When we think of it, any suggestions on story movement, diction, and so on, given regarding our creative works have largely been beneficial to the other.

We quite often enjoy reading all good poetry, and can share the poetic vibrancy of Silvia Plath, W.H Auden, Theodore Roethke and Wole Soyinka. Nhamo can still be found gleaning over the pages of Marechera's poetry, while Joyce reads anything that comes her way, although it wouldn't be strange to find both of us sharing Alexander Solzhenytsin's works.

Our reading tastes are rather different, with Nhamo favouring serious fiction and non-fiction works and Joyce reading voraciously whatever falls into her hands. Nhamo can read Russian novels, Guy de Mauppassant, e.e cummings, and so forth, but is also comfortable with political and philosophical works such as V.Y Mudimbe's *The Invention of Africa*, Kwame Appiah's *In My Father's House*, Malcolm X's autobiography or Frantz Fanon's *Black Skins White Masks*. Joyce prefers to read Science Fiction and any other speculative writing, but as said above, she will read any printed material including bottle labels!

To Nhamo poetry is the most compact way of expression. His poems are vignettes of what he experiences as an individual, which he then tries to refract as of public importance. Socio-political historical events are also an easy raw material of his rather public poems, whose strength perhaps is the ironic twist and sardonic touch in the narrative. Joyce's poems are rather cerebral and very private that she appears to be addressing her own soul. She is comfortable to approach the public from a purely private space, as a mother and sister forced by painful circumstances to face an unsavoury reality.

Zimbabwean poetry over the decades has been a way of capturing the nation-state coming into being with all its inadequacies, prejudices and ecstatic self-discoveries by poets when they see their individual selves as unique prisms of all that constitute either colonial Rhodesia or postcolonial Zimbabwe. We are more acquainted with Zimbabwean poetry in English, although we know some totemic praise poems and other new publications such as *Tipeiwo Dariro* written in Shona. The poetry of Chirikure Chirikure in Shona has been inventive and stimulating, and some of it was made easily available through adaptation into recorded popular music, such as Oliver Mtukudzi's rendition of 'Kanyanisa' (Mix up). The poetry of anthologies: *Zimbabwean Poetry in English* by Kizito Muchemwa, the racially representative and comprehensive *Mambo Book of Zimbabwean Verse in English* by Colin and O-lan Style, Musaemura Zimunya and Mudereri Kadhani's *And Now the Poets Speak*, Chenjerai Hove's collections, alongside Freedom Nyamubaya's *On the Road Again* and Chirikure's Shona works can easily be a way of visualising the existential conditions in colonial Rhodesia right into contemporary Zimbabwe. It is possible to read them alongside the purely academic history texts and get a much more vivid understanding of the events, processes, sensibilities and values that have been at play in the country. Unfortunately, the depressed Zimbabwe situation over the last decade has not seen the publication of comprehensive poetry collections in the country.

Another anthology would probably fill the void, although online poetry websites have helped to rectify the situation. Here we think of arts journalist and writer Wonder Guchu's *artsinitiates.co.zw* and Emmanuel Sigauke's *munyori.com*. Sigauke's website is an international platform for poets from all over the world, but has significantly featured Zimbabwean poets who otherwise would not have had their work recognised elsewhere. Both of us have been featured there. The South African arts and culture journal *KOTAZ* also made a commendable feature of contemporary Zimbabwean poetry, with a diverse range of poets from the elderly Julius Chingono to new entrants such as Tinashe Mushakavanhu. However, outside print published poetry, Zimbabwean poets have performed their works, especially locally at the Book Cafe in Harare, and internationally at poetry slams and festivals. Names that easily come to mind are Chirikure Chirikure and the protest poet Cde Fatso, and of course exiled Chimurenga popular musician Thomas Mapfumo, who unfortunately failed to get a visa to perform in neighbouring South Africa at the Durban Poetry Africa festival in 2008. The problem of travel visas has restricted the performance of Zimbabwean artists in some countries across the globe, with Nhamo failing to perform at the Dambudzo Marechera memorial celebration at Oxford University. British immigration officials cited that on the "balance of probabilities" Nhamo was most likely not going to return to Zimbabwe, in view of the cholera epidemic that was then devastating the country, as well as the collapse of institutional structures due to bad governance.

Does Zimbabwean poetry have hope and a future? Yes, indeed great works are coming along. New names are already appearing in anthologies, especially on poetry websites; names such as Tinashe Mushakavanhu, Zvisinei Sandi and Christopher Mlalazi. In our own home, of our three children, Tawanda, our youngest teenage son, has already penned some stories. Whenever he lays his hands on the family computer he makes cartoon animations or he writes imaginative fiction. That alone is encouraging to see someone take after us without any direct tutoring or conscious urging from us as parents.

Nhamo Mhiripiri

INTERREGNUM:
THE SHORT SLEEVE OR LONG SLEEVE CHOICE

The cache on the roads is hard-times
The talk is about empty shelves and hunger
A gnawing calm shrouds the nation, protected
From real and imagined imperialist intrusion
Wise old men chide forgetful youth who hunger for alien sugar;
They thank revered ancestors for dividing the vote
Protecting heritage so righteous patriotism wins the day
We walk like stunned ghosts in reverie
Hunger itself is a mind altering non-substance
We can't believe the horrors we have survived
As chauvinism took up arms in defense of priviledge
In the name of the motherland at correctional *pungwes*
We sing, dance and sloganeer; more than half of us acting out
Hearts congealed with fear; worried stiff anyone can testify they
Saw you celebrating change after March 29 election.
The verdict is predetermined - machete passes on
And it's your turn to make a choice on which of your hands
Dared touch the untouchable profaning war memories
Putting an insulting X on a people's ballot paper
To please British Blair
You think of your wardrobe - which shirts number more:
Short-sleeved? Long-sleeved? The answer helps
Choose which arm is axed short-sleeve or long-sleeve length
A warning to vote wisely next time if we survive starvation
An existential signifier never to sell out land;
Never disrespect graves of our selfless dear departed
Always remember to clench that one fist, punch the air,
Chant with unquestionable vigour – *"Pamberi neChimurenga!"*
Hailing living ancestors who always know
What's right for the nation.

WHEN YOU MEET MY COUNTRYMEN

When you meet my countrymen at airport terminals
Those who shuffle uneasily and are timid about visas
Those that are quick to tell you they're visiting a relative
That tell you the Z$ isn't worth the paper it's printed on
And swear cheekily in the same breath about Uncle Bob,
Corruption and a botched up land reform programme,
Just know they may never go back home given half a chance.
When you meet my compatriots on a journey,
Those that are fast to tell the media about political violence;
Talking in a staccato like men on the run,
Who duck shadows and see the state spy network
In the coffee they drink on flights to Gatwick or New York,
When you meet these dear countrymen of mine,
Who have one million and one stories of abuse
Each grisly enough to earn refugee status at immigration;
Who tell you they are activists fleeing for precious life,
I tell you when you meet them just be a bit wary.
Some of us can con you out of your sympathy.
Just be careful every one of us abroad is a political refugee.
We never talk about our debts or child maintenance fees or
Criminal cases that for some are a more serious danger to flee
Than a cannibalistic despot that eats its own citizenry.

IN AFRICAN GULAGS

They wail out in fetters
Gasping for freedom
Sucking in the little air let in by shackling laws.
They scream to rent the man-made silence
So that neighbours and watchdogs move in
To plead on behalf of sanity.
They lament for the relaxation of over-taxed states,
Where workers struggle on unholy pittance,
And collective action is deemed anathema
While capital power is supreme right.
Plaintive cries are answered with whiplashes,
Bludgeoning batons, canister gas, and dingy jails of steel.
In the ensuing confusion, sympathetic intervention,
Bleary-eyed, is lost in apoplectic sneezes.
And some, perhaps still well-intentioned,
Find sanctuary at cocktail parties,
At V.I.P receptions with sumptuous meals,
Hosted by spin-doctors from Ministries of Public Relations.
They sup on snacks and diplomatic talk
On rule of law and public order.
The worst are won over with whisky
And state employed sex workers
So they forget what they came for.
The tense air outside still feels rationed.
The best amongst them recollect themselves from the hangover,
And at least they go back to the world
Having written damning reports on atrocities
In dictatorships that prop up run-away gravy trains.

J. Tsitsi Mutiti

LEAN THINKING

Isn't it absurd?
Those who have the most
Strive the most to work with less
What comes so naturally
To those who have not

It has of course been our lot
To be the ones they make
More out of less from;
Ten years ago their pound
Bought ten of our dollars
Then five years ago
It bought a hundred
Now it buys hundreds of thousands

In those circumstances,
Do you need anyone to teach you thrift?
Cholesterol is bad for you
We hear
Well if you can afford enough
Cholesterol for it to harm you
You're well off don't you think

Sugar in excess will damage your health
They say
But the energy now needed to get it
Will just about balance
The energy out of it

Coke will dissolve a tooth over night
We hear
Well here's a dental headache solved

Coca cola
Relocates disinvests or
Whatever the current buzzword for deserting your former hosts
Like fleas off a dead dog

Look around you
And you'll see that
Borrowed tools are not dependable
Oh have we forgotten our
Ancient wisdom in the rush to be a part of
The new age
The global brands
Chanting
"Just do it"
"Obey your thirst"
"J Lo"
Across the globe

Abandoning ancestral wisdom
Has its price;
Living forever on the sufferance
Of those who heed theirs
And on the capital of our children's
children's children.

TO GIVE AND NOT TO COUNT THE COST

Little boy
Sitting glumly in class, sighing
Thinking maybe if you're good
They'll bring back your teacher
Maybe they'll untorture him

Little girl
Working glumly at home, sighing
Thinking if you're good
They'll return your mummy
And put her together again

Little boy
Little girl
Big boy, big girl
All equally distraught
Bewildered, wondering
Did you have to go that far
Just for a bit of ink?

Wondering why
That X has to be so dear
Wondering why her brother's
Is the blood that must atone
For whatever sin resides
In a misapplied X
Wondering if this is how God felt
When it was His one and only Son
Who with his blood was to atone
For all the world's sin

But at least, he was resurrected
Little girl, little boy

Be brave, be strong
No amount of goodness
Will ever untorture or
Put mummy together again

Now we begin a new life
Of doing without the luxury
Of a mummy or daddy
Brother, sister, cousin
Friend, whatever

Of doing without expensive, damaging
Luxuries, like revenge
Like resentment
And living in the past
Or feeling pain for the
Immense wrongs done
To our beloved ones

Little brother, little sister
Be strong, knowing
Our nation being born in blood
Is dammed to be built in blood
Knowing when we pride ourselves
In the bloody nativity of our nation

It condemns us to constant re-enactments
Of those bloody scenes
Knowing that sweeping
Accountability
Under the carpet for the sake of peace
Only buys us more tears
In the future

Hearing about hope for
Future glory
Bought through the lamentations of many
Hearing about being realistic
And wondering why

It is more realistic for those
Who commit the most heinous crimes
To always earn the reward of impunity
While those whose lot it is
To be the blood donors
For the nation building project
Find themselves alone and outside
In the cold?

Emmanuel Sigauke

THE ORIGINS OF MY POETIC JOURNEY

Poetry is like a companion that I turn to at the most crucial moments. It is a vehicle for my deepest feelings about life. In 1990, after A-Level, I turned to poetry during my temporary work search. I had just discovered Dambudzo Marechera's poetry after reading his novella, *House of Hunger*. Poems like "I am the Rape" fired up flights of imagination and the more I read them, the more I wrote. My poetry at this stage was more like journal-writing; it was not for publication, but to occupy my free time. In addition to Marechera, I also read British classics like John Clare, Thomas Hardy the poet, D.H. Lawrence, a handful of the Romantics; I particularly adored William Blake and John Keats. I regarded the poets as companions in interpreting the language of life.

Throughout high school, I asked my friends to listen to my stories and poems, and the smiles that would light up their faces fuelled my efforts. As a sixth form student I was active in my school's writing club and I managed to network with Vitalis Nyawaranda, whose book *Paida Mwoyo* we were studying in Shona literature. I had met him at a writing workshop in Harare, and he immediately became my mentor. He commented on my works and encouraged me to send them to publishers, which I did. The works were politely rejected, but I liked the salutation "Dear Writer", which was on most of the rejection letters.

When I arrived at the University of Zimbabwe (UZ), I had written hundreds of poems, which amounted to nothing, but I managed to re-envision some of them and prepared a manuscript entitled *The Voice of Silence*. UZ introduced me to African literature courses, which were like a reawakening because I was taught to view African writing seriously. I discovered Wole Soyinka, Okot p'Bitek, Chenjerai Hove, Charles Mungoshi, Jack Mapanje, and many others who wrote about the realities of colonial and neocolonial Africa. Knowing that poetry could be based on what mattered to my people's experiences was liberating. The poetry in *The Voice of Silence* was not art-for-art's sake anymore, content was more important than form, and the poetry used phrases like "my people", "the workers", "the struggle" and "voice of the voiceless". One poem that represented the sentiments of my newly-discovered role was entitled "Like the Poets", in which I made a list of all the African poets who influenced me. I tried to capture what each represented.

Mudereri Kadhani and Musaemura Zimunya's book, *And Now the Poets Speak*, helped in the affirmation of my new role. I sought to show that I was a responsible writer through my writing, but there was still a part of me that wanted to write like John Clare or Dambudzo Marechera, a part that wanted not to care about society, because some of my early model poets had presented the individual as more important than society. I wanted to let the strength of the poem anchor on craft. Then I discovered Chinweizu's landmark book *Towards the Decolonization of African Literature*, which helped me understand the ambivalence that assailed the African writer. It showed me that African literature was torn between the need to gratify foreign audiences and to remain true to the African experience. Not only was I supposed to write for my people, I was expected to write in my mother tongue—Shona, or in an English that could be understood by the common people. Ngugiwa Thiongo's *Decolonizing the Mind* had an answer for me: Align with the workers, speak for the voiceless, write first in your mother tongue and translate later. Then I read Chinua Achebe's interviews and was reminded that the writer was a teacher, a role that came with great responsibility.

At the UZ one of my classmates read everything I wrote—everything—and he wrote reviews of my works, making clever claims like "Sigauke is the chronicler of society's hard hours." And I did that exactly. I remember a poem I entitled "Taken Advantage of", which was about a poet that no one paid attention to, an observer of the ills of his society. My reviewer read the poem and wrote, "Sigauke is a voice in the wilderness." He said I was a visionary who saw what others did not see. Friends like these were a great influence in that they validated my efforts and, of course, fed my sense of vanity.

The defining time for my aspirations as a poet was when I participated in the Budding Writers Association of Zimbabwe (BWAZ). I learned that poetry came to life on the stage. Nearly everyone who came to our workshops in Harare performed poetry and looked serious, like a "chronicler of society's hard hours". There was Albert Nyathi, the first chairperson of BWAZ, who had already established himself as a national performer. His electrified stage appearances inspired a lasting desire for performance. I wrote several poems (Shona and English), which I memorized and performed in schools and libraries. Each performance was an act of revision, which led to better written versions of the poems.

BWAZ exposed me to other writers and it created a sense of community I had lacked. When I became the publicity secretary for the Harare branch, I played the role of mentor to other aspiring writers, and I learned some secrets of the craft. Shortly after, I became the organization's national secretary, a position that came with nationwide travel, since we were establishing branches across the country. My signature poem, which I performed at every BWAZ function, was a Shona piece called "Yauya Shanduko", about the 1992 economic hardships in Zimbabwe, when the IMF-mandated economic adjustment program had taken a hold and people were losing jobs. The poem captures what in another poem I would call "the heart attack of a new era". It, together with a follow-up poem entitled "VepaSpeed", was recorded by Aaron Chiundura Moyo at the ZBC Radio 2 and was broadcast nationwide. This led to more writing and confirmed that, indeed, I was a "chronicler of society's hard hours".

A HOUSE FOR MOTHER

It's a shame we never finished mother's house.
The plan germinated on Independence Day;
then we left the village and settled in Harare -
occasionally returning home at Christmas
to sleep in mother's rickety hut.
It's a shame we never noticed
the village's embrace
of the new solar-lit homes, frowning at our grass thatch
that pricked the village's pride and exposed our backwardness;
so one December day we moulded concrete bricks
dug a foundation, hired a builder,
and left for the city where we owned
too much furniture in other people's houses,
where we brushed shoulders with eviction.
A big house back home
would be our validation
and mother's pride.
It's a shame we never finished that house though;
Now mother sleeps under the glaring sky
in a roofless half-walled apparition, blanketed by the moon,
scanty taste of how it would feel
to be in a real house, which would be complete by now
had we not left the village
to hide in the city, away from village whispers
and the bushes' muffled laughter.

THE VILLAGE MOTTO

Fists splitting skulls
Children born not to listen,
Now hammered to sense,
panel-beaten to nonsense;
The day was new
The day was new
The day was new.
Eucalyptus man, guardian of lambs.
The sun kisses whip. Trees fold arms and pout
Rocks of Chisiya and Chigorira weep
As they line up for treatment. Now heaps of whips
Shall travel and bulldoze drains in supple flesh.
How can they let the cattle
How can they let the cattle
Stampede Murowa's maize field?
Mopane whips Fury's twins
And legs tear the air
As the troop of children escape terror
But Terror's breath licks the earlobe,
And before it's too late
Another adult arrives, then another
Circling the little convicts
Who must know what it means
For a village to pound sense
Into tomorrow's leaders.

BULAWAYO AND OSLO

I don't want to talk
about those days of little explosions
at Mototi when the buds itched
and the chases began, toothless, smashing
into granite walls of rejection.

Let me talk about Bulawayo,
where I chased her scent
after she left our village
swooped by the eagle of distance.

Only Hope's messengers
forged words of courage, making me wander
like Tukano's lost dog, until I
found myself shivering in an Oslo office.

Suppose the Bulawayo sniffle had
nodded her voracious "I do",
what would Oslo be confessing

had I not made it to that meeting
where one word over tea
gave birth to a new possibility,

when you told me about the snow
and I told you about abundant heat
and you praised the wonder in cold

and I sang about the thunder of the sun;
then you mentioned centers of knowledge
that surpassed my corridors of wisdom
and by the end of the night you and I
you and I, you and I, especially you and I!

In my office, standing behind me, you peer at my progress,
asking: what Bulawayo, what Mototi?
Had I stayed the course of that original chase,
tell me how you would even stand here
and say, "Honey, remember to log off."

GONERA BEES

Don't tell me about bees
and expect to see joy
that anticipates the harvest of honey.

Those Gonera bees in Chigorira hill
knew when to descend
and puncture the peace of our compound
landing wherever was surface:
liquid, solid, soft, and hard -

Oh, don't forget
that they knew how to find your eye
knew what message to send
to anyone who crossed their way
which was everybody
who might have forgotten
the joy the bees got
just buzzing in our ears,
some with suicidal joy
planting their stingers in us
if we acted aggressive,
whatever that meant to a worker swarm
away from its hive;

so don't mention bees at all;
don't mention honey or the money you can make;
don't change subject to wasps either.
The hill, the cave, the hive,
and one boy running
pursued by an angry swarm
and you get the idea.

SMITTEN WITH ART

She stood outside the bus window.
Face—cliff of affection—seeing
Me off to Harare, moments after
The encounter with her razor-sharp auntie
Who told her to squeeze commitment out of me
Before I left the house:
"Take his jacket, watch, or briefcase."
Niece in veil,
Sliding down church aisle,
Shuffling up the slope of validation
"These crooks harvest and vanish.
This one will cross oceans, dip
Beak in strange bowls and forget."
Out there she stood
Eyes of doubt locked with mine;
Ears listening for confirmation
Of the dreaded departure.
I will always dream about that stare,
Will embrace the talons of beauty
Dancing in the golden smoke
The brush strokes of a Sizinda sunset.
Will she blame her aunt, when she
Remembers that day, or the airplane
She never saw whisk me away?
She will remember the sunset,
Whose fiery art captured the wings,
Released them when the handle snapped
And ink smudged ambition's canvas.

Christopher Mlalazi

THE TIMELESSNESS OF POETRY

Poetry for me is an outlet for the thoughts of that inner fool who is not easily accessible to the outside world. That inner fool who is the careful contemplator, who takes their time to shape their thoughts, and when the thought has taken shape, who also wants to imbue it with beauty, to make it palatable even to the gods, no matter the language used or the message that is contained. I might be saying 'up yours' to somebody whose ideas I do not like, or saying I love you to somebody's wife, and that all done on a harmless piece of paper or a microphone as in the spoken word, but whatever the medium, for me careful and conscientious craft of the art is of paramount importance, because at the end of the day what poetry seeks to do to nature and the universe is akin to what Angels give to life – harmony. We have written stories, we have hammered stones, we have moulded mud, we have produced drama, movies, grand spectacles in the sports, but for me the underlying principle in all these activities is mankind's often feeble attempt to emulate the beauty within. Poetry is like a flower growing on the tip of one's tongue, a dainty little flower that seeks to lend colour to our whispers with its fragrance and settle the tremors in our hearts. A world without poetry is like a song without tune, only fit for the refuse dumb. Poetry is a confirmation for humanity that we are in tandem with nature, that we have the ability to laugh, to sing, and above all, to love despite our differences. Poetry is timeless, and within that timeless void it is a bright star twinkling in the firmament on a summer night, guiding our dreams to their mark.

Oftentimes we stagger around in life bewailing our lot in this existence, believing that the gods have not been kind to us, that life is harsh to us, and forgetting to open our eyes and minds and behold the ripe fruit of poetry that grows all around us, only waiting for us to raise our hands, pluck it down and squeeze its refreshing liquid between our lips. There is no balm on earth that is more soothing than a dose of poetry. Even the first cry of animals as they are brought to life is poetry to the judicious ear. The eye sees poetry, the ear listens to poetry, the tongue tastes poetry, the finger touches poetry, and even the nose smells poetry. The sun is poetry, the wind is poetry, the moon is poetry, and so you too are poetry. It is for that reason that on some stormy summer nights when we are safely cocooned in our bedding and the rain is pattering on our roofs, we often have the desire to grow wings and fly above the thunder and lightning to the space beyond. It is poetry calling to us.

Even when a bolt of lightning strikes, we sometimes have the impulse to be part of the bolt, because it is an exhibition of the might of this poetry that is our lives. We have seen grandfathers and grandmothers in villages around fires in the evenings, drunk from that opium of eloquence, we have seen heroes being praised, we have seen our children on moonlit nights playing hide and seek, we have seen lusty lads on moonless nights stealing across the village led by their amorous hearts, and all this done for the love of poetry. And then who said that poetry is the pursuit of the mindless? Who said that poetry is the pursuit of the vain in heart? Just show us that person today and we will tell them that they were bewitched by poetry! So let your heart sing, just as we sing when we are coming from *ebhawa sigave amabele*. It is that easy, just flow with this river.

A SOUNDLESS SONG

A frozen wave from the roadside
Between the dreamy trees marching backwards

A goat mercilessly tearing
At the petticoats of a tree unable to flee

Bloated cows crunching mouthfuls
Of helplessly trembling verge-side grass

A boy-man sitting on the coiling trunk
Of a fallen tree gone dry
Plucking on the fishing twine strings
Of a tin banjo
A soundless song for you as you drive past

WHERE WILL THEY BE ON XMAS DAY?

As our children
stare wide eyed
at glass cases of sweets
that their poor fathers
can no longer afford to buy for them
to sweeten their Xmas days -
where will the *shefs* be on that day?
As mothers patch old clothes
that their children can cover their buttocks
and their husbands their crotches
between their perforated trouser legs
as cockroaches threaten mutiny
inside bare cupboards
faced by the beautiful face of hunger
in houses where once voices laughed
on sunny Xmas days -
where will the *shefs* be on that day?
with their looted public funds

THE WORKER'S FLAG

Still they trudge
Homeward bound
Alongside the highway
With the eye of the red sun
Peeping at them from the western sky
As it prepares its blue bed
For its children the merry stars
To come back home
And rest their silver sparks

Home is a long way
If the stomach is empty
After a long day of toil
Behind monsters of machines
In the echoing factory
That threaten to maim limbs
As they produce
What the machine operator
Will never afford to purchase

Still they trudge
Homeward bound
It is a long way home
If steep slopes separate it from work
That must be negotiated
As they rise and fall
Blow and billow
And the weary body is burdened
By thoughts of debts
And hunger and anger
As to the west
The twilight sun sets
Its colours the country's flag

WHEN WILL THE SERPENT SHED ITS SKIN?

A country peeling
Old crusty skin
Lovers and haters
Plucking at the drifting flakes
Blown before
cynical currents
Trying to patch tattered dreams
That still
In their gaunt eyes gleam
Like unflinching agate
In sun and wind-blasted
Mute deserts

THEY ARE COMING

Gogo watches timorous
through a rent in her curtain
as the kids boil down the street.
Minutes ago
a terrified woman ran past
bleeding, dress torn,
yelling: THEY ARE COMING!

In an instant the streets were empty
of even the wind
only the yelling
cadres of national sovereignty
wielding dread in upraised little fists
like that man they admire
on the front
of their T-shirts.

Gogo fears for her only son
she told him not to go –
but leaving
he told her "the country will never be a colony again".
He is leading the *toyi-toyi* towards her home
sweating faces set
feet pumping
stones and sticks raised
teeth bared
with intention.

Josephine Muganiwa

NOTHING FOR FREE

It was a mad day
Their eyes were red
Lips dry and cracked
Determination written on their faces
The delegation had been mocked
They could still hear "his" laughter
"Nothing for free, nothing for free
Communalism is dead.
Only survival, think survival."
To answer your greeting, present money
To give directions, present money
To receive feedback from "him", present money
Then the women and children caught on
To be sent to the shops, there must be a 'cut'
To cook the daily meal, present money
To clean the house, present money
No one child did anything without being given money.
Everything came to halt in the district
Someone passed by, reported to "him"
He came and announced a meeting with a loudspeaker
No one attended because he had not paid them
He paid a few, including the delegates to attend
He stood on the raised platform and shouted slogans
No one responded, he had not paid them
They had lived out his advice
For the first time in years, he apologised

SENIOR PASTOR'S CONFERENCE

It was the mother of all conferences
Only the great tones were invited
They came with their wives
Those without wives brought Personal Assistants
There were two registration desks
It was presumed:
    One for the males
    One for the females
Not that it was the original criteria
But it seemed interchangeable
She was late, and so the queue had cleared.
The first session started in twenty minutes
She rushed to the desk, pen poised to sign
The lady at the desk smiled and smiled,
    'Hello, are you a pastor's wife?'
She smiled curtly, shook her head, eyes searching for register.
    'Oh, you must be a PA then?'
Again she shook her head, smiled, threw a glance at her watch.
    'Oh...' the other lady was at a loss
By then she had scanned her name
Picked the register, signed
Smiled sweetly and walked into the conference room
Staring at the register, the secretary looked stunned
    'Pastor Henew is a woman...yet so popular'
Stocks of her bestselling books lay in a tray
Without a photograph at the back.

Ignatius Mabasa

THE LANGUAGE I CRY IN

Inspiration

I have made several attempts to write creatively – but there is something that I have discovered in my writing. Inspiration almost always comes to me in my mother language – no matter where I am. I have tried to convert the lines that have come to me in my native language into English to try and please as well as show those around me that I am a writer across languages, but my lines in English are never the same as they come to me in Shona.

I have had the opportunity to occasionally work with young writers in the Budding Writers Association of Zimbabwe (BWAZ). My main job with BWAZ is to help upcoming writers improve their writing through workshops. I have realised something in all the years that I have worked with these young writers, and that has made me reflect on inspiration and the language to use when writing.

Wrong Language

I have read a good number of manuscripts by young writers in Zimbabwe and have reached the conclusion that there is talent in the country, but a good number of the young writers are writing in the wrong language. You see, the cancer of colonialism has spread in Zimbabwe to such an extent that most people feel it is fashionable to speak and write in English. Yet, the sad thing is that a good number of Zimbabweans will never be able to tame that 'foreign' language. It takes a few exceptional individuals like the late Zimbabwean writer Dambudzo Marechera who once said of his use of the English language – "I took to the English Language the way a duck takes to water." And indeed his use of the English idiom shows that. I have many a time been asked by my own people – why do you write in Shona especially when you have travelled far and wide? I have not found a clear answer, and I am still thinking of an answer to this question.

The Language I Cry In

There are so many reasons why I write in Shona, which is one of the two main languages spoken in Zimbabwe. I have spoken the language from birth. It is the language that I think, dream, cry and laugh in. Because I have this language that I do not have to fight with when I need to express myself, I feel it is folly for me to try and express myself in a language that does not come to me naturally. I feel I am not talented with the language in the way Dambudzo Marechera was. For me, writing in Shona is liberating. When I courted my wife, I did that in Shona and I still remember the conversation very well. All poetry!

As a student, I spent three years in Norway doing my Masters and after that I went to the United States for one and half years on a Fulbright Scholarship to teach. One thing that I still vividly recall in those years abroad was how tired I got after being a slave to languages that were not my own, languages that have their own rules. I missed very simple things like *Kwaziso/Ukubingelelana* on the then Radio 2. It was when I was in Norway that my award winning novel *Mapenzi* was born. I suppose I did not have problems writing the novel because after spending the day listening to Norwegian and talking in English, the characters in my novel would take me back home and would talk to me in a beautiful language that I understood. The novel became a means of escape from English and Norwegian, from the isolation of language.

My novel allowed me in the coldest of Norwegian winters to slip away and join my folk at my grandfather's farm where I grew up herding cattle and was in constant touch with the soil, trees and insects. The novel allowed me to revisit stories I grew up listening to that featured Hare and Baboon as the main characters - a fantasy world in which animals interacted with human beings but reflecting real-life situations in the human world.

Childhood Influence

I think that one's childhood plays a big part in how you develop as an artist. What I write, and who I am is mainly a result of my interaction with the thick bushes, the imposing Pfura and Mavhuradonha mountains, their barking baboons, the rivers – the fragrances of nature and the carefree laughter of women coming from the well to fetch water, and even the lowing of a cow that has been separated from its calf as the sun goes down. The beauty of my people's language brought out through the storytelling evenings, the riddles, proverbs, songs, dances, games - all so difficult to anglicise are so dear to me.

My first serious attempt at creative writing was in Shona when I was in form one. I remember classmates accusing me of having plagiarised the story I had written for the creative writing exercise. Fortunately, my teacher defended me and challenged my classmates to bring the book from which I had plagiarised the story. Instead, my Shona teacher asked me to go and read my story to teachers in the school staff room. I still recall my tiny voice silencing about fifteen or so teachers who were in the staff room. That experience gave me confidence, and ever since I have felt that Shona is my language, that I can do and say what I want, how I want it.

As I continued exploring writing, I used to also read a lot of Zimbabwean novels in Shona and English. I vividly remember the beauty of Shona novels especially those written by Charles Mungoshi and Patrick Chakaipa in particular. Mungoshi has a special way of telling stories in a very simple manner. I also recall that because of my love for Shona.

Dilemma

We are faced with a dilemma in Zimbabwe. We speak and write in English alongside our indigenous languages, but we can't be called masters of the English language or even our mother languages. English is a foreign language which we love and abuse so much. Besides writing in Shona because it is my language and I love it, I think that the experience I got while assessing manuscripts for the BWAZ made me feel the need to help young writers de-mystify the language.

Most budding writers feel that if you write in Shona you are not worth talking about. Besides, most of them have been to schools that make it a punishable offence to speak in any other language than English. Yet, one will see that a lot of these young writers may show flashes of brilliance, but lack the ability to enslave the English language to say what they want to say. Sadly, it is not just the English language, but also their own mother languages. The grammar, spelling and poor sentence construction is shocking. The result is what Alan Paton stated in his novel *Cry the Beloved Country* that – the tragedy is not that things are broken, the tragedy is that they cannot be mended. Despising our languages in preference for English has become institutionalised such that undoing it will need a good policy that will have to have been implemented yesterday.

SWINGS AND SEE-SAWS

In metamorphosis, the caterpillar triumphs
Yet I wake up the same toad, un-kissed.
Orphans, child-soldiers and rape victims ask,
Is bliss as defined by the *Oxford English Dictionary*?
Agony plays on creaking swings and see-saws
Hoping one day the children will return.
Darfur, Mogadishu – I want to feel your pulse
I want to know – is it concussion or rigor mortis?
Our incestuous consciences are in menopause,
A brother chosen is closer than a brother born.

CAVITIES

That woman, the mother of Nyevero
Has a tooth that needs a filling.
Her husband has been in London
Since Nyevero was 2, now she is 7
Who can blame the mother of Nyevero
For having so many cavities?
Mai Nyevero, carefully chooses her seat.
She sits carelessly opposite me,
Exposing wads of tan thighs, and grins
"Look Mhizha, the forest is full of trees
But your axes are old, rusty and blunt"
She winks at me, gathers her skirts and swishes off,
Laughing like a happy hyena in the dead of the night.
Night finds her in bed with that fool Gandari.
But woman, Gandari was caught last week
Naked in bed, with the new teacher's wife.
This Aids – python, myth or phantom
Will surely finish us all off.

CONCRETE AND PLASTIC

I miss the open air
In the open fields.
I miss the stretching space
That was usurped
By high rise glass buildings.
I see ashen street kids
Playing and fighting
For an inflated used condom:
"Strong, dependable and
Can hold up to 3 litres of water."
I look around me
For the coloured butterfly
And the soaring eagle,
But the city has created
Urban modern birds.
The candy eating pigeon,
The hamburger-munching crow.
I miss the human being
In all this concrete and plastic
Where robots and computers,
Professors and talk-show hosts,
Telemarketers and experts
Tell me what is best for me
Even if they don't know me.

DEFIANCE

Defiance is when
The skies are
pregnant with
heavy grey clouds.
Defiance is seen
When lightning grins
Menacingly to earth
And thunder bangs
On earth's door
Saying, open, open.
And yet
No drop
Of the sacred rain
Kisses the sad, dry
Dying wrinkled lips
Of the earth.
And the old farmer
Shakes his head
Tucks his dirty hat
In his armpit and
Limps home.
His shoes crunching
The toasted corn plant.
The 3rd Chimurenga is:
A different kind of revolution
No heroes, no merit, no medals.

POETRY

Poetry is a white child
Lost in the darkness of a cinema house
Holding my black hand
Calling me daddy….

Phillip Zhuwao

... AND LOVE WEPT

Morning cloud has come
Will you be under its shade?
It's like I'm watching this city
Under an angel's siege
Its like I'm watching
Narcissus holding himself.

I've seen death's nobility over all
I've seen the incest of two cities
And I've sensed adultery's shudder
and the night's voice
darkly

"Where are you?"

But of this
I've seen nothing
But

I'll wait under morning cloud
and catch the descending tears
pretending they are hope's victory
over those sad truths
...and love wept.

WHEN THOUGHT REMAINS

Between us this wall thickens
and
Promise's whisper is silenced
Where can we hear
The laughs of innocence
and
The trusty pats on shoulders
We remain
one two islands
bridged by this water
to become
dots from heaven's Sight
Two gulls' droppings

MAYAKOVSKY

Is that Vassilisa
Hanging on the pylon
my
How the snow is deep today
Poor girl
How ugly she's turned

left at the Crimea
is this widow's love
that I see today
as the gun's spittle

The poet spoke
of Akhmatova's moving lips
Rasputin, naked
diving in the deep snow.

THE JAR OF CHRYSANTHEMUMS

Gold overwhelms that purple in the Sun,
Her shades on the table and
Breakfast's coy smile

"Have you slept well?"

HUSH HUSH (HARSH) MY LOVE

It's
When I'm alive that
I'm afraid of Deth
(don't forget)
        the sand's blackmail
        the
          Ostrich's head in battle

they are many writers by the fireside
When pine logs crackled
forebodings of the dark's shadows

the 2 of us know
I won't stop you crying
no blood can fertilize colonised soils
deth is deth heroes burn in hell

longtime back we cannot
mention legends and executioners
Who said
        Poetry should not be corrected

this ocean mingles with the orange river

Cirrhosis blinds my eyes
but
the
muse
bids me stand on hill top -
        the grasses are vales Savanna dew
        my black brotha discriminates me
        When bullocks fight

      and lo is between those horns
      what chance do I have

    I like every man -
Jew or gentile
      love
You know me thru and thro
      was I politik those nights

Madness of me Cruel
I seem to talk to you
as if you smile before me

are crystallnachts these lullabies
that premonition granny's pregnancy

I've packed my bags every hour
yet my destination
seems
not to know me

On the doorway (hush
We are 2 lonely strangers (hush
Is the eagle decided to land (harsh

We no longer contemplate
I here
Yu there
as this continent
becomes a doormat
where angels make violent love
annointed by my blood.

Tinashe Muchuri

FIFTEEN MINUTES DRIVE

bored by bad music
from a commuter omnibus' radio
his elbow squeezed my nipple
he made my day
though I did not tell him
our custom forbids that.

MOTHER'S PRAYER

God
I did not know
that, my daughter preaches
love in church.
As you know God,
everything I wear
was donated by neighbours.

RUNNING AWAY MEN

running away men plunder
on their way to asylum
innocent children endure
the rampage.

GUEST OF HONOUR

They imagined
A guest of honour in suits
He came in rags
They drove away
Later they learned
He was a freedom fighter

A SOLDIER'S CONFESSION

In the name of my leader
I betrayed them
I detained them
I lied about them
I tortured them
I killed them.

Ruzvidzo Mupfudza

POETRY WOOS

I started writing poetry as soon as I started to write prose. Third grade. I was more concerned with the rhyming scheme than anything else. I remember winning a third class poetry certificate for a poem on the environment while in the fifth grade. From then on, my fate was more or less sealed.

There was a stage of rap-poetry in high school, and a lot of it was influenced, believe it or not, by LL Cool J. Then in university, there was a lot of love poetry, written for many young women who I fell in love with in a Van Gogh like way - tragically most of it was unrequited love. Thankfully I never had to resort to cutting my ear to prove that supposed love of mine.

Studying Shelley, Wordsworth and other Romantic poets at A level had a lot to do with it. Then actually, watching the movie *Dead Poets Society* and hearing that the purpose of poetry is to woo once again sealed my fate and subjected a lot of innocent women to bad verse!

Then second year at university, back in '92 we came across Literature and Socialism - all of sudden the whole question of art for art's sake versus art with a cause became a battle ground where most of our dreams died. After reading a poem in Harare's First Street during that year's Zimbabwe International Book Fair (ZIBF) which I think was commemorating Dambudzo Marechera, I began to doubt the usefulness of poetry written in English and read to a public that had their own first language. I seriously considered giving it all up and crossing the Limpopo and joining my Azanian brothers to fight for their liberation. If words could not flower in a fruitful way perhaps bullets and blood in the name of liberation could.

In the end I resolved it all through more writing and drinking. It was grist for my poetry, you see. Through poetry I sought, like Charles Mungoshi, to refine my prose. I even went into advertising to learn the art of minimalism - to no avail.

One day reading traditional Shona poetry, courtship, love and all, I realised that for better or for worse, I too, was a poet, just like my forbears, and my subject and style would vary according to mood, place, experience - and now it seems age. So over the years I find I have written about the futility of life, the joys and terrors of hedonism, the ugliness of political stagnation and also the hope of love and the power of the human spirit. Do I contradict myself? Perhaps. And why not, artists are Legion by nature, and we cast out each particular demon with each peculiar outpouring of the Muse.

QUEST

In the deep of the night
I go looking for stray pieces
Of my broken soul
Sojourning through the sub-terrain
Of Harare's temples to Bachus
But all I find are more shreds
Floating across the ragged face of time
I grasp at shadows dancing
In the hellish light of the night
Paying homage to gods of booze
And sordid commerce
Our libation is the beer pouring out
Of the broken bottles that shatter
To the floor when they slip
From our sweaty and sleepy drunken hands.
The incense we burn is our money
And good sense.

A BINGE AT THE CROSSROADS

We sit, perched on our barstools
Like mushroom-satellite dishes
On Hararean roof tops
We desperately try to cling to our youth
But age has the final say
Our minds are not as sharp as they used to be
To be sure, through the haze of cigarette smoke
And the fumes of booze we glimpse ghosts
Of our younger selves but we turn away our beer-soaked faces
We drench the walls of urinals with our creativity
Sadly, fleeing the shame, we signal the waitress for the next round
Resigned, for it's obvious we're going to be on the stools till
Dawn breaks

ZIMLIFE

We're haemorrhaging as a nation
Take a leaf out of the Zim-dream
And its texture will be a nightmare

Our hopes ooze down sewer drains
Falling like the Zim-dollar
Crumbling into a fist-full of dust

We walk down the street
Clutching our dreams
In a wad of lotto tickets

Counting the hours until Saturday comes
Dreams are sweet in the midst of the nightmare
Till it all evaporates with the announcement of the results

OUT OF WHICH THE MAFIA IS HEWN

In the tormented and tortured silence of our grief
The ancient rain tree silently weeps
Shedding dry tears that do not drench the earth

Uhuru stands crucified
At the crossroads of a new world disorder
Nehanda swings and blows in the winds
Lynched on the tree of free enterprise

As the narrative of our nativity unfolds
There wise men from the West
IMF, World Bank and Europa
Come to dig the gold and oil out of our souls
Wining and dining with sons of the soil
Judas Iscariot
Selling their own brethren down the river
For a modern day case of whiskey, shiny beads and all

For how long shall the ancient rain tree stand
Dry and dying while the palms of the drummer bleed?
Our rainmakers in their suits and white collars
Can only summon dry rage
Still dreams clog the air
We plant our memories in the graveyards of strangers
While we watch foreigners rape our mothers
And the ancient rain tree does not bear water anymore

You look to the west expecting to see sunrise
And the ancient rain tree will shrug
Refusing to bear water anymore
Until you return to the old country
And reclaim all your sacred places, pools and hills
Discarding the diseased condoms

You wear around your minds and soul
Only then shall the voices of stone
Disdain to speak to you again
And the impotence of the ancient rain tree
Shall come to pass so that earth and heaven
Can for all eternity, hold fecund conversations again

SONGS OF BONES

I'm dreaming Nehanda swinging
Strange fruit in Hararean breezes
Speaking to standing, watching, ancient trees
Talking, eyes shut, seeing
The phoenix resurrection
In a war dance of freedom

I'm remembering Nehanda deciphering
Signs and portents of bones
Flaming letters carved in the stone of defiance
Her children forever singing
Redemption songs borne of ancient wisdom
Restless spirits walking the land until it's done

I'm looking at the ancient tree standing
At the centre of dreams and memories
From whence the roots of our stories
Grow, the trunk of our being reaching
Out to the distant skies and stars,
Undying bones, laughter through time's tears.

Zvisinei Sandi

IS GOD A WOMAN?

They say God can be no woman
'Tis not for woman to be so cruel
Not for her to crush life before the ripening
Nor for all the world, torture a sinless child

Agony, soul destroying, bewildering agony
An angry, defiant, disbelieving child
Exacting, unforgiving, unrepentant.
Demanding eye for eye and tooth for tooth

Is God then uncaring, a Mugabe, a villain?
To whom the lonely, suffering soul matters not?
Must have multitudes to stroke his vanity
Yet will crush the innocent without a care?

Hush! Hush child! God is God should it matter.
God is compromise, compassion, Love.
Mother's love, that makes breakfast from the air –
Love, that builds a life out of tears.

EXHORTATION

I said it to you, yet you did not listen
I tapped your shoulder, you paid no heed
Look now, as all falls apart
Pay heed as your head is smashed in.

How many days have passed hence
Since the moment I told it to you
How long, how long, brother of mine,
Till the day you hear my voice?

For the long snake does not bite its own tail
And the father eats only a little
He leaves some crumbs for his children.
Brother of mine, you rip open the belly of the crib!

Rumbi Katedza

AN OPEN LETTER

We fell in love the first time we met.
I was newly born and you were timeless.
You were with me when I said my first words
and took my first steps. You watched proudly
as I learned to ride a bicycle and caught me
every time I fell. You were there on my first
day of school and comforted me with your
strength when I ran home crying after
I had been sent home for not paying fees.
You quietly examined every suitor
who came calling for me and soaked up
my tears with every heartbreak and goodbye.
My successes were yours and yours were mine.

You were there at the airport the day I left
to seek out greener pastures, and somehow,
thousands of miles away, I still felt you close by.
The further I went the louder you called,
beckoning me back to your cradle. I heard your
cries on every radio and television newscast.

There was pain in your heart as I kept my back
turned, enjoying the fruits of far off lands.
You continued to comfort others, as you
were trodden on, abused, ravaged and raped.
You had the painful responsibility to witness disease
and atrocities and then bury our people in their thousands,
Slavishly cleaning the dregs of predators in suits.
And still you continued to comfort those left
behind, while also encouraging us all to grow.
Near or far, we were all your children.

You embodied so much promise, but now you

seem so tired. Your fatigue makes me tired,
and so I continue to search for home. Yet still
I hear you calling me in newspapers, magazines
and books. There is no limit to your reach.
You always manage to find me. I ignored your cries
for as long as I could, but eventually I had to face
my fears and return to your bosom.

You are my past, my present and my future.
You are my parent and my friend. You are my first
true love and you will be my last.

You are my yearning heart and my fragile soul,
my very breath and my fighting spirit.
And all I can bequeath to you is hope. For in you
lies our children's future. You are me and I am you.
You are my home. You *are* home. You are ZIMBABWE.

LAST DOLLAR

The night bird calls with many voices
Calling its disparate flock to arms,
Leaving those who hear with ever few choices,
Urging all to fly, for its cry doth disarm.

Sitting at dusk in his banged up old Sunny box,
Waiting in line to pay government his last dollar
To pass one of their new makeshift roadblocks
That had his neighbours' pockets noosed by the collar,

A whooping cry suddenly came from this motorist
As he realised: *I have no more blood to give!*
You've sucked me like a vampire terrorist.
If I give you one more dollar I cannot live!

He hadn't been home for many a day,
Not a single penny in his pocket to pay for passage to
His own home less than two kilometres away.
Now that he had the money, he knew what he would do.

He disembarked his car with his wife and children,
Leaving it to its own fate beside the big 'T' sign,
Blocking the single lane, knowing full and well that when
It would be towed, he would accrue an additional fine.

He was resolute he wasn't going to pay any more money.
And his twenty-year-old Nissan was close to death,
So he would walk home now with his hungry family
Without turning back to waste any more breath

On those who would unjustly charge him for the right
To go to his own house. He would not pay for this blight.

His children would all tell this story, for
All their days, as long as they would remember
The day their father refused to pay a dollar
At a toll gate to go home sometime in September.

The night bird calls with many voices
Calling its disparate flock to arms,
Leaving those who hear with ever few choices,
Urging all to fly, for its cry doth disarm.

Masimba Biriwasha

ONCE UPON A BLOODY JOURNEY

Once, travelling in ragged Zimbabwe
Heartbroken, head pounding
As if a thousand madmen had run amok
All fuelled by propaganda's machinery
I saw a drunken fight
Two men sprawled and kicking
Each other on the ground
Head-bashing and blood-gushing
Next to a bus filled to the hilt.
Now I was sober like daylight
And couldn't make why the country had been dragged
Into a cesspit.
When I saw the first man rise up
Spitting blood, a crack above his eye
With his tongue lolled out, he screamed:
"When will freedom come?"
People shook heads in agreement
And in that moment, I saw Zimbabwe
From Mutare to Victoria Falls
Draped in the people's blood.
And of all the things on that journey
That's all I can still recall
A country torn apart
Its people soaked in blood
Like the two drunks fighting to death
Over a political slogan.
Maybe that senseless fight
Was the beginning of the tearing
Down of the walls that divide us.

WOOD

My foundation is of wood,
The thick colonial type.

It screams hollow when I step on it,
It shines smooth when I sweep it.

It reveals stains within its layers
Stains that rise like smudges of black blood.

Its core is a harvest of thorns
Its skin is painted with wrinkles of wasted years.

Its veins are as aligned as a famished choir
Singing disjointed choruses of oppression.

Yesterday I scrubbed it till it shone in the sun
Then it exploded carrying me within its soft embrace.

Towards a new leap of faith,
Towards freedom, O sweet freedom!

Togara Muzanenhamo

THE CHRONICLES

They still drew the old roller over the cricket pitches with men
yoked like a team of oxen to the stubborn iron wheel.
The grass smelt as the grass did, all rich beneath the afternoon sun -
the heat flashing to the ground with a blinding flick of steel.
All the fields were there - but much smaller than remembered -
the rugby and football grounds unused, the whitewashed lines
washed out by the rains, but the names of dead Jesuits, on signs,
still stood on the preened edges - in traditional white and red.

Up into view the memorable tower of stone rose with all the dreams
of climbing up the winding cool stairwell, up to the top of the turret
where thoughts of fields, soft with warm breaths of red top, met
the sky with hope and refuge. But those were just a schoolboy's dreams
brought on by the sight of the huge bronze plaque of St. George
plunging his spear, extinguishing our fears of the dragon.
Though all that bullshit vanished with age, the staged hero on the forged
plaque still remained some old myth the Jesuits liked to work on.

'I'm here to go through the Chronicles.' '86 to the mid 90's.'
The receptionist is grey and half-deaf, I'm apparently soft spoken -
so there's a lot of repetition accompanied by grimaces and apologies.
'I'm here to go through the Chronicles.' 'Yes', to another question,
'I did attend here some years back.' 'Yes, an Old Georgian, an old boy.'
The phone slowly goes up to her ear as she mentions something
about visits and strange requests from foreign journalists wanting
to sit in on classes or have private interviews with the boys.

'Penny?' 'Yes, Penny it's me'. 'I seem to have a safe one here.'
'Wants to go through the Chronicles.' 'Something about poetry.'
Her small eyes look up. 'You do remember the way to the library?'
I had forgotten, but then retrace the steps in my mind to get there.
Each class I pass, a voice spills from the mock-Edwardian windows,
the red polished floors tap under my feet, and a sweet blessedness

fills me that I'm not sat in those sweat-rooms of learning, shadows
of my youth, daydreaming about a new-world after the first kiss.

The study-hall has lost all its desks and holds an array of instruments
and chairs for classical musicians. The fountain in the quad is gone now,
and at first it didn't mean a thing to me, but then a crude bewilderment
took hold when a memory tried to find its place in the absence; and how
on earth they removed it had me lost - the lawn was perfectly smooth.
The weights' room, where our hands were beaten blue by a leather wad,
where iron was pumped on hot afternoons, was now clean and had
the smell of sweat and leather replaced by veneered internet booths.

Outside an office a boy lifted his hat and said 'Good morning' in a way
that had me question what he'd said. It was only when I looked back
that I noticed the strain on his face, his rheumy eyes and the big black
words scoured across his chest, FAGGOT. I could see how easily they
could have pinned him down. The tree was there where we sat at break
trying to forget the colour bar that still hasn't faded outside the gates;
the smell of *musasa* leaves and old orange peels revived a dead ache
that filled my belly: a mob outside the science-labs, fists of other kids...

When I met Penny she smiled, and something told me
it wasn't a strange request to come here and go through the Chronicles.
She had them stacked up on her desk, all piled up chronologically -
towers of memories, names and dates in black and white at my disposal.
I sat down, leafed through the pages, the photographs alive in my head;
and after an hour of being immersed in the vivid quiet, the bell rang:
It was still that same high-pitched drill that once brought relief as it sang
through the long corridors, but also brought with it a certain dread.

AT MEASURE

It's the dreamy air that will send you off to your death,
the dark silence stoking amber light in the distance.
And you're heading home, the car droning along at speed,
that safe speed that keeps your blood warm and cradles
your heart. Your foot's steady on the accelerator, every
peaceful thought you own kneels at the altar of your being.

Stars play accomplice to the magic of small villages,
neon lights hurtle by without sound - the names of towns
flung into the glass depth of your rear-view, where
everything vanishes. Fourteen hours straight at
the wheel, in three hour's time it will be her birthday;
you'll walk silently into the house, slip off your shoes,

climb the stairs, undress, then slide into bed with her.
You'll make love, and stay up till dawn embraced in the age-
old gesture. Through West Nicholson to Colleen Bawn,
the darkness parts out for you, the car slips through time.
On the seat beside your own: a veined roadmap of South Africa,
a small velvet jewellery box, a bottle of warm red wine.

A KILLING

It took almost thirty minutes to herd the bulls
into the kraal. The sun blazing off their hides,
all black, burnished, unmarked sculpted muscle.
Their dark eyes shone, their nuzzles glistening,
refusing the dry pallor of blond dust rising
from the ground – the earth's mist dissolving
somewhere above polished sickles of horns.
For a while a dance of shadows and death -
hooves drumming into a mad chaotic ground,
a frayed, careless rope flung like a dirty halo.

Some cowboy-playing man, swinging his hips
for a laugh, swung the lariat again. Onlookers
bowing with laughter missed the fluke catch.
The rope gripped. With each movement came
a refusal tightening at the base of the bull's
horns. Six men fought a tug-of-war for another
fifteen minutes. Cracked feet grated baked earth.
Bellows and pure force reared in disagreement –
to the rope, to the crowd, to the man standing
by a car wearing overalls, holding a simple axe.

BUYING OUT THE DEAD

for Isabel Manuel

First come the old with spectacles lodged halfway down their noses, squinting at cardboard price-tags on dusty antiques. It's the odd things no-one really uses that go under the hammer first: the large plastic typewriter, the *Capzil* fan, or various recordings of classical music on audio cassette. Near amateur stamp albums, a dark business works the eyes of men sorting through worthless coins and war-medals. But it's all about lot 372 - pre-federate stamps marketable to Gibbons

or the bald man around the corner from Covent Garden, the man who spends his days dreaming about retirement in Fresnaye, listening to 702. Once a month, an old yellow-and-black sign reads 'Auction' outside the Senior Citizen's Club. In the hall, an assortment of belongings fills the air with a barrage of flat perfumes and blunt domestic scents. An elderly woman smokes and talks to two other women; she has a fruity cough, her fingernails - a burnt custard yellow, she sells viewing tickets and catalogues like a bored ticket clerk in a boring art gallery.

On display are some belongings of people she knew - not necessarily friends, just people she casually spoke to. Lounge suites and sofas, cabinets and beds: furniture's the eeriest thing when it comes to buying out the dead. Everything with fabric is tainted, everything in the hall is fractured and will fracture further with new histories: a young man and pregnant woman stand by a scarred wooden cot, silver-plated cutlery lies tarnished black in a worn blood-velvet case, faded mirrors strain the reflection of my face as I gradually accept that anything glass here

is rarely clear, and anything solely wooden is the best untainted thing I could buy. Old books and vinyl lie untouched. There are no bronze nudes here, or oils on canvas that could be called anything close to anything worked. It's all just ordinary stuff left behind from ordinary lives. If anything precious is found, it missed the sharp eye of inheritance.

The dead were sent elsewhere to die; and here in this sixties-styled building, the months come as the days sort through the hours of our lives.

AMNESIA

Mimosa come alive with chatter, dusk's reverse
manner calling with cockerels. Children's laughter
surges, folding silk red shrouds of dust over a game
of football. Nearby, goats stand on a trough sipping
water, the backdrop: a fallow field with the silhouette
of an old green engine, the sun hauling amnesia in.

Men with heavy heads and greased overalls walk
past like ghosts to cramped houses fucked with smoke.
Saturday's done, a gallon of sun dumbs wives' screams,
wives praying for the fresh dawn walk their children
take into fog-layered fields, singing songs through
gilded sheets of sunlight. The walk to Bryn Farm

for school. But now the goalposts of rapoko stalks
defy all natural laws and stand. Instinctively the goats
make their way to the pens. The sun sets. All that's left
on the horizon are hazed silhouettes of children being
swallowed whole, their laughter subsiding, a red
bruise turning black fast where the sun went down.

Batsirai Chigama

ALIEN

I am gone yet I did not leave
Somewhere, sometimes
Pictures of home vaguely traipse
On the dance floor of my mind
A single pirouette cut in mid air
Gone

I feel at "home" in a land not my own
In my thorn infested home
My bed adorned with prickly pebbles
I can't sleep, so I leap

Bound for the unknown

POEMS IN AN ENVELOPE

I found them faded, forgotten
With cockroach stains
Stamped on warm words
That began and flowed without end
Lying hopelessly in your old school trunk

Written for Eustina
The girl whose beauty captivated
Bees in flight and reduced their sting
To a sweet stillness in midair
Suspended, hoping they too
Would hold their hand like you did

Words flowed from the past
Into the life I live with you
Scars of old paint pictures
On stained paper without reverence
Of the carats I thought bound
You and me, faded yet so alive
The dying poems in an envelope
Addressed to Eustina, not me.

BEAVEN TAPURETA

WALKING 'N TALKING

When I wish to be free like the birds
I think too much about the future
I am always walking 'n talking
Always on the shift
Searching for something I cannot find

What I want to be is not what I am
I am a meandering wanderer
Where can I freedom on a Sunday morning like this?

I am afraid of the world outside
Something out there goads me off balance
And drops my soul in the dark abyss
Alone here, there, everywhere
I learn to shelter myself in the dark

I think too much about being in love
What is the answer to love when
Love is a numeric dilemma?

My feet fall over the barbed ground
On the road to a destination I know not of
Humming a song slit by sorrow:
I am the uprising sun of tomorrow
I am the moon
I am the star that shall win tomorrow

WORKER'S DAY

As the sun shoots over the horizon
We put our tools down
Go home fagged out, time wilts into dreams

Every day
Go home after work
Every day
For a month, like insatiate bees, males and females
Go to and fro
Calling ourselves workers
For the whole damn month
And what do we dig up?

The sun rises
Colouring our sweat-smeared faces
Tools injure our hands
Our backs go limp
Yet here we go again
Unpaid
Unheard
Unwanted

Every day
We wipe our tears away
We hope for a month
And what do we dig up?

Me the security guard
Protect I protect
But I am not protected
Him the teacher
He teaches but all he is taught
In return, is how to be broke

Her the nurse
She nurses the future with uncertain
Hope
Them the builders
Build palaces but their homes are pyres
And others, being artists, don't get their dues
O workers, arise, arise!

Cosmas Mairosi

THE LORD IS MY SHEPHERD

the lord is my shepherd
I shall not want any other leader besides him
(even from his own party)
I shall have no other political party besides his
I shall not suffer any domination by the British or
the Americans
and my country shall never be a colony again

the lord is my shepherd
even if I walk in the valley of freedom
I am forced to attend his rallies
I shall not say what I want
because the police and the military will descend
on me

even if I walk in the shadow of poverty
I shall continually shout his name and sing his
praises "long live my leader"

the lord is my shepherd
I shall not associate with members of the opposition
I shall not walk with demonstrators
for should I be found out
I shall be beaten or tortured

I shall have no other TV stations besides his
I shall see what he wants me to see
I shall hear what he wants me to hear
I shall read what he wants me to read

the lord is indeed my shepherd
I shall not starve

for I shall certainly be given food handouts
to vote for him
and other people's land for free
squatting

but now the lord is not my shepherd
I have suffered many setbacks
my business operations have been closed
my bank accounts frozen
my house has been demolished
my land has been confiscated
and unto me a new law hath been given:
"thou shalt praise the lordship in all his follies".

AMAI CHIDO

Amai Chido, my wife
when you are tired of dancing before the minister
when you are tired of chanting slogans
and brandishing placards
when you are tired of attending rallies late into the night
and putting on slogan-branded apparel
please come home, I need you
by my side.
the children have since grown lawless
my nights have become too cold
the homestead itself has become too dirty
the crops are dying un-harvested
the livestock has scattered in every direction
I know you are fighting for a noble cause but when
you are tired of trading insults with your opponents
when you are tired of tearing down
opposition strongholds
when you can no longer stand the battering,
the hiding and fighting
when the hype and the adrenalin is finally over
please remember me, my love
the children and I need you home
Amai Chido.

STILL THE SAME PEASANTS

we are still the same peasants
scarred by yesteryear battles
scalded by the colonial *sjambok*

we are still the same peasants
who sang at the *pungwes*
and cooked for the comrades

we are still the same peasants
who sheltered the once courteous freedom fighters
we who implored the spirits of the land to look after them

we are still the same peasants
who cheered when *uhuru* was attained
who clamoured at the downfall of minority rule

we are still the same peasants
milling to the rallies with our hungry bellies
still unable to send our children to school

we are still the same peasants
watching the fat politicians flash by in posh cars
leaving us their dust and disdain
we are still waiting for our share of the gains of independence.

VISIONS

I saw visions
crucified on cinema walls;
a crippled economy balancing on expired bank notes;
political slogans forced down children's throats;
freedom manufactured into a delectable dish by
hooligans and despots.
Visions.

FREEDOM

I saw
freedom written on terrestrial walls
freedom written in children's blood
freedom oozing from decaying bodies
I heard freedom's anthems sung by decapitated souls
and mothers reaping the severed limbs of their
toddlers.

I saw
fathers' hopes going up in flames at the height of
civilian demonstrations and political protests
freedom distorted in the jumbled hysteria of
wailing widows
freedom frozen in the mouths of bantering dictators
freedom summarised in endless fear and pain.

I saw
freedom ending in political turmoil and
economic slavery
babies abandoned by dollar-seeking mothers
corrupt officials farting on embezzled donor funds
democracy failing to remove dictators from the
throne
and the people growing used to such oppression.

I saw
all this slander and bloodshed and
said, "freedom is here, mother!"
but then demented like drowning shadows
all the free turned on me and said,
"we have reaped nothing
of what we have sown."

NoViolet Bulawayo

DIASPORA

we perch like lost doves
on frosted branches
of alien trees whose names
we don't know
lands far away from home,
we are the strange fruit.
we laugh into our armpits
so we are not heard,
walking like the winds
breathing like stones
to stay unseen.
like starved mongrels,
we run to unwanted jobs
we mind crazies, clean poop
break backs, push, shove, anything
we will do anything
to western union money home
to waiting, famished families.
and sometimes dizzy for the homeland,
we google, we facebook, we msn
we log off, hang our heads in pain,
sleep with eyes wide open,
and dream in tears.

INDEPENDENCE

She came dressed to kill,
Liberty, a whore spotting a green-yellow
red-black-white georgette,
the men came from the war
and put their weapons down,
kids crawled out of hiding places,
women birthed children named Hope
named Freedom named Elizabeth,
aunties slaughtered chickens to cook
over demonic fires in celebration,
black girls and black boys took
to the streets *toyi-toying*, chanting
Amandla! Viva! Mayibuye iAfrica!
but that was before the whore got up
one night and sneaked away with a lover -
an old man on a rattling red bicycle.
Today we look for her in each other's faces,
bleeding and heartbroken, clutching
posters that read "missing".

BALANCE

I have been to London
to look at the Queen.
Also been to the motherland
to look at mama. The Queen
can not do without her glasses,
sitting and looking at nothing
and other things. Mama's eyes
have never known any glasses,
no thank you, looking at the earth
of rock, as she bends back broken
in a red field, sick child strapped on,
singing of the war next door,
the Aids in my brother's home,
and praying for two rain clouds,
while waiting for the government
to send her pension that's overdue.

DARFUR

whose blood is this that baptizes the wind?
this blood, also splattered over that black river?
whose soul is that? that soul, twisted
like a red face towel and stuffed into the muzzle
of a gun, just whose body was this skull attached to?
this long skull that looks a little intelligent? Excuse
me, but whose beautiful child was that? her long legs
hacked off and left frozen in scattered flight
towards a reddened road, whose? this red empty shoe,
ah, it's a Gucci, but whose? if you don't know,
you don't know, I'll let it slide, like that pitch-black
body over there, sinking head-first into a dungeon,
slide, like the odour of screams and fear that just passed,
if you don't know then I won't ask no more,
just pass the coca-cola, cheers comrade, today
we wake up again to the fatal poetry of fat, green flies
high on shit - the diarrhoea of bloody machetes
is also the stench of a pregnant corpse's head
flung far back against a still-born Darfur moment
in case you missed Rwanda, just in case.

SOUVENIR

blackened blues cling to the sealed lips
of women, weary of absentee husbands
and lovers busy working black bended
backs in the dark mines of Johannesburg,
the women become faithless child brides
of time learning to love it while we become
the lengthening shadows of our fathers,
we are the children of the men who fled
Zimbabwe for South Africa's mines,
maybe to return and maybe not, who knows,
leaving behind newly-born human tokens,
still souvenirs clutched tight clutched deep
around the stomach in fatherless husbandless
nights, we are the haunting drumbeats of hijacked
moments between tattered sheets, we are discord
tunes lulling our mothers with hopeful hopes
of their returning, overdue soul mates while our hands
are frantically trying to hold our sprouting
heads down so we do not grow up to follow
the long-faded footsteps of the fathers we never saw.

Emmanuel Sairosi

SOON THE TRUTH BECOMES APPARENT

Soon the truth becomes apparent
Turning back would be out of question
Ahead lies the battle point – the Limpopo
To tell you is to taint you
Those who have lost their children
To lands beyond and afar
Only when they see the Limpopo
Only then can they understand
The world in the manner
Their children interpreted it
It is not just a myth
The Limpopo has robbed us
Thousands of future leaders
Lured by the treacherous symphonic waters
Limpopo smells blood
Limpopo smells victory
Limpopo a two-faced conniving brute
Limpopo were you not supposed to be the epitome
Of the life we so deeply yearn for?
Limpopo you have ruptured the veins
Of hope entrenched in our utopian world
Undeterred and exhibiting fearful braggadocio
Limpopo you glide like a serpent
Squaring up and ready to devour
Unsuspecting karoo lambs

Kudzai Ndanga

SONGS OF TRUTH

I am no more.
I am the song of boy soldiers
Filled with the favour of bloodlust.
I am the song of the child-bride
My legs spread open
For the erect members of greed.
I am the song of a mother raped
By her son as he attempts to go back
Through where he came from
In hope of being born again.
I am the song of the guns they hold
Like guitars in their hands
Loud enough to deafen their ears to the pain.
I am the sound your crisp US dollar makes
As you sell your soul on the black market.
I am the song of the grandmothers
Tsk tsking their tongues in tune with
The chaos this man 'Politics' has brought with him.
I am the song of the earth turned red
From too many fallen souls
Whose sacrifice does not appease you
Red earth that clings to the feet
Of those who tread upon it
Singing their endless songs
Whilst looking up at the sky
And ignoring the truth that speaks to them.

I AM NOT MY MOTHER'S DAUGHTER

I am not my mother's daughter
She was born to the sweet beat of independence
Her mother's heart full of hope
Named for the struggle, they called her Born-Free

I am not my mother's daughter
I was born to the cries of freedom
Hope a distant memory long turned ash
Born into the stench of a dying Zimbabwe

My mother's desperate hands pushing me
Away from her dry, diseased breast
Into the great Exodus to lands full of promise
Named for the loss, they called me Diaspora

Tinashe Mushakavanhu

WRITING FROM THE OFFSIDE POSITION

When I left Zimbabwe to study in Wales, I wanted to experience something other than Africa but the contrast set me off balance. Zimbabwe seemed so remote and stone-aged and the reality of the political crisis became even more apparent. I could see what we were being denied, the crushed dreams, the unfulfilled promises, the stunted growth. And yet, the new environment could not appease me.

Nestled in the Welsh countryside, I lost sense of my positioning in the world or even that such an idea was an important resource for a writer. And yet, places have always informed my writing, my awareness of self. My earliest sense of location was in a series of Harare poems I developed working with the British poet, Steven Waling, during the Crossing Borders Creative Writing Project, a British Council and Lancaster University initiative which paired us, young African writers with experienced mentors in Britain.

The Harare poems grew beyond me. Harare was a living organism, constantly changing its appearance and its mannerisms. Harare was the conniving character with my visiting muse. The creative urge for me then was to capture the life around me; its complexities, its absurdities and the simple daily happenings. Here's an example of a poem inspired by a moment walking in the belly of Harare:

ENTREPRENEURSHIP

A faded signboard
Posted on our sagging fence
Reads:
WE DIE FADED JEANS
But on the gate
Instead hangs
An exhibit –

> A threadbare napkin
> Soiled and holed
> A flag of indigenous
> Entrepreneurship
> Waving our poverty
> To passer-bys

This is a poem about the everyday and how it's surreal. It's a poem that sings to the poverty and deprivation of a city. But, once I left Zimbabwe, I could not dream to write like the old me. I belonged neither here nor there. My poetry became the changing comment of my own life experience. Zimbabwe remained an important place to which even though I was not physically present, I frequently returned to imaginatively in my poetic creations. Zimbabwe intruded into this island of comfortable exile, violently and almost annoyingly, especially when I still had family and friends living there.

Living in exile, I ceased to be myself and my life thereafter became a negotiated existence. In the new environment, there were many collusions and contradictions; many peoples, many languages, many cultures encountered. I realized that sometimes the enemy is outside the self, everywhere sites of struggles. I no longer had a country. I didn't want no country. My country became the whole world because where my heart lay, there was my home.

TOMORROW IS LONG COMING

Homesickness is a bird that sings to dawn
While it's dark. Is the tree outside a forest
To itself? Or time frozen in obeisance?

And yet the distance between you & sleep
is somewhere between your nerves and
the cold sheets.

Beneath your bed the rodent of exile whispers
'I'm just another rumour spread by loneliness,
I'm not real, I'm not real.'

THE DISTORTED LOOKING GLASS

From the bedsitter window
I watch them walk down the road
Arm in arm clutching Tesco carrier bags
They pretend the world is one big stop-
shop without suffering and pain

They saunter sway jog laugh
Up and down Waun Burgess Road
As if they can enjoy the sunshine
Of youth forever and yet they will not
Let the world know for fear
Of their delicate skin

IN THE HOUSE OF EXILE

This town I have adopted
Snoops at me suspiciously
Veiled in the colour of its skin
Blind to my dark presence
Only the green of nature
Breathes out clean air

I look homeward and see no angels
Heol Pentremeurig is too narrow a road
As parked cars crowd the street of my life

Perhaps exile is only skin deep
Memories of home time will confiscate
The deep freeze of history

This town I have adopted
Cobbled streets, here, everywhere
Is the masonry of centuries past
The search draws me nowhere
Near kindred spirits

In this town I have adopted
"I'm the incredulous sneer
Tucked beneath bland smiles".

CROSSING THE LINE

We entered the Friends Arms holding hands
The way Jesus and Judas must have been
When they both knew each other's secret

No words, my coal black hand tightly clasping
Her long white fingers but it was the silence
Drawn in turned heads and suspended gestures
A haunted hush, an odd clink of glass, a cough

She and I had gone down Taboo Valley and
Crossed River Prejudice, that led up to this spot
In Love's sacred paths

Michael Tsingo

SOVEREIGNTY

Sovereignty where is your propriety?
All I see is murder, destruction and poverty;
Sovereignty where did you come from?
On whose loose tongue do you froth?
Was He that invented you ever on the frontline?
Sovereignty how can your comrade say 'There is no crisis'?
Sovereignty if there never was a crisis
Then where is the national currency?
Is this not the highest display of insufficiency?
Is this not the result of extravagancy?
Sovereignty if there never was crisis then where is my opportunity?
I am tired of being a nonentity living in pity
I don't eat a government-of-national-unity!

Abel Dzobo

CITY BLUES

Immaculately caparisoned people
Sashaying down the street
Spectacles seemingly chasing ghosts
Shiny shoes radaring the pavement
Jewelry decked anatomies
All moving boutiques
And him? His scarecrow-outfit billows
As he jumps from the concrete mattress
His tar complexioned torso
And bitumen-cracked skin
Outstretches charred hands scarred
And like a truant
He furtively telescopes around
Slowly grabs the bin lid, the city refuse
He, the societal refuse
Anticipating the day's meal
What have they got for me today?
Ah, a mound of petrifying morsels
Typical palatable half-bitten nibbles
From Noah's ark of salvation
He smacks his emaciated lips
And takes a handful
No! Hey! Wotcha doing? Voetsek!
He turns around
The immaculately dressed shadows
Knock the food from his mouth
Take away his bin, burn the contents
You will contract diarrhea, this is dirty food.
Disgrace! They move on.
He is now alone. Starvation or diarrhea which will win?
His tummy rumbles like the grunt of an Aberdeen Angus.

THE ZIFA CHAIRMAN

Not even the City Engineer
Knows Harare as I do
City Centre to Warren Park
My nose and forehead
Not even the Mayor
Bulawayo Road
From Zesa House to Jameson Hotel
Five potholes
Roomy enough to swallow six puppies
Jameson to Caltex Service Station
Four oilrigs
Then ZANU PF Headquarters
Dinosaur-fist induced abysses
Nine jagged cauldrons
Not even the Town Clerk
From ZANU PF Headquarters to the Showground
The annual Harare Agricultural Show
Have dug up 13 spitfires
Just hope it's not a Friday
A pity, no zeros to slash
Showground to OK
Then ah, the National Sports Stadium
12, the disciples
Gaping at the Chinese handiwork
Not even the Director of Works
And now the Heroes Acre
The Taekwondo jab to your car
Seventh Dan belt
Gawk at North Korea's masterpiece
Up to the Warren Park 1 junction
Quarter of an hour brutes
I said not even the Mayor
I am the ZIFA Chairman
Zimbabwe Footer's Association Chairman.

Notes on Contributors

JENNIFER ARMSTRONG b. 1968 in Harare (then Salisbury). She is close to completing her PhD on the poet Dambudzo Marechera. She loves adventure – skydiving, scuba and freestyle martial arts.

MASIMBA BIRIWASHA b. 1975 in Zimbabwe. He is a children's writer, poet, journalist, social activist and publisher. His first published book, *The Dreams of Stones*, was awarded the Zimbabwe National Award for Outstanding Children's Book in 2004.

NOVIOLET BULAWAYO b. 1981 in Tsholotsho, in the Matebeleland region of Zimbabwe. She's currently a postgraduate student at Cornell University in creative writing and was highly recommended in the 2009 PEN/Studzinski Literary Award for her story, 'Snapshots'.

BATSIRAI CHIGAMA currently works and lives in Harare. She is a poet, short story writer as well as interested in film. Her work has been widely published in South Africa and Zimbabwe. She's an active member of the Zimbabwe Women Writers.

JULIUS CHINGONO b. 1946 on a commercial farm near Harare, and has worked for most of his life at Zimbabwean mines as a rock blaster. His only novel, *Chipo Changu*, was published in 1978; an award winning play, *Ruvimbo*, in 1980 and a collection of poems and short stories, *Not Another Day* in 2006.

ABEL DZOBO b. 1984 in the eastern city of Mutare. He graduated with a BSc Hon degree in Media and Society Studies from the Midlands State University. His writings aim to expose and ridicule the societal ills of his day to public attention and tries to find solutions to existing problems.

JOHN EPPEL b. 1947 in South Africa and raised in Zimbabwe where he still lives, making his home in Bulawayo, near the Matobo Hills. He teaches English at Christian Brothers College. Some of his books include: *The Giraffe Man*, *The Curse of the Ripe Tomato*, *Spoils of War* and *White Man Crawling*.

CHENJERAI HOVE b. 1956 is a self-exiled Zimbabwean poet widely known for his NOMA award winning novel *Bones*. He has published extensively on Zimbabwean politics, culture and literature. Some of his books include: *Shadows, Red Hills of Home, Shebeen Tales, Palaver Finish* and *Blindmoon*.

AMANDA HAMMAR b. 1959 in Harare, Zimbabwe and holds a PhD in International Relations. Her doctoral work and subsequent writings have been linked directly to the changing conditions in post-independence Zimbabwe. She regards writing and reading poetry as essential to her well-being.

RUMBI KATEDZA is an award winning writer and filmmaker who has lived in the USA, Japan, Canada, the UK and Zimbabwe. She has worked as a radio presenter/producer for a popular Zimbabwean station, formerly Radio 3. Now an independent producer and director, she directed the Zimbabwe International Film Festival (ZIFF) for three years. Her fiction has appeared in *Women Writing Zimbabwe* and the BTA/Anglo-Platinum Winners Collection.

IGNATIUS MABASA b. 1971 at Karanda Mission in Mt. Darwin and grew up at his grandfather's farm. He is deputy director at the British Council Zimbabwe. He is a performing poet, novelist and story teller. He became a household name with his trendsetting debut Shona novel, *Mapenzi* and recently published a second, *Ndafa Here?*

COSMAS MAIROSI b. 1977 in Mudzi. His parents divorced when he was six and his father died when he was seven. He grew up in the custody of an uncle and aunt who supported him through to Seke Teacher's College. He is a primary school teacher but still finds time for writing and performing poetry. Some of his poems have been published nationally and abroad.

DAMBUDZO MARECHERA b. 1952 – d. 1987. He grew up in Vengere township, Rusape, which provides background to his first book, *The House of Hunger*. He died of AIDS complications. Best known for his eccentric behaviour and no-holds-barred attitude to life, his works are widely studied in Europe. His publications include: *Black Sunlight, Mindblast, Cemetery of the Mind* and *Scrapiron Blues*.

NHAMO MHIRIPIRI b. 1968 and grew up in Harare and Chitungwiza. He has published critical works on Dambudzo Marechera. He has short stories in *No More Plastic Balls, A Roof to Repair, Creatures Great & Small* and *Dreams, Miracles & Jazz: New adventures in African Writing*. He teaches at Midlands State University.

CHRISTOPHER MLALAZI b. 1970 in Bulawayo. His has published a short story collection, *Dancing with Life* with ama'Books and a novel, *Many Rivers*, with Lion Press in the UK. His play, *The Crocodile of Zambezi*, co-written with Raisedon Baya, was banned and won the 2008 Novib PEN Freedom of Expression Award.

TINASHE MUCHURI is a poet, performer, actor and writer currently living in Harare. He performs regularly at arts festivals in Zimbabwe and currently features in a local historical soap called *Tiriparwendo* as the character, Jecha. His poems are featured in *Illuminations* (USA), *Rattlesnake Review* (USA) and an anthology *Jakwara reNhetembo*.

JOSEPHINE MUGANIWA lectures on literature in English at the University of Zimbabwe. She writes short stories and poems and has an interest in gender issues in language and literature.

CHARLES MUNGOSHI b. 1947 into a farming family, and raised in the Chivhu area. After leaving school he worked with the Forestry Commission before joining Textbook Sales. He has written novels, short stories and plays in English and Shona and often considered as the 'granddad' of Zimbabwean writing for his prolific output. Some of his best known works include *Coming of the Dry Season, Waiting for the Rain, Stories from a Shona Childhood, Kunyarara Hakusi Kutaura* and *Ndiko Kupindana kwaMazuva*.

RUZVIDZO MUPFUDZA lives and works in Harare. His short stories have appeared in *A Roof to Repair, Writing Still, Writing Now* and *Creatures, Great and Small*. Some of his stories – creative and journalism – have also appeared in national and international publications.

J. TSITSI MUTITI born in Mt. Darwin. She did her primary education in Gweru and Concession before going to Harare for her high school education at Arundel School. Though she has no "arts" background, she reads widely, classics and science fiction. Some of her short stories have been published in *A Roof to Repair*.

TINASHE MUSHAKAVANHU is a 'bornfree' whose first cry was *ku*Gomo in Harare. His childhood was a series of movements in the 'locations' of Harare until his parents found a home in Gweru. He writes across genres. He has appeared in the *Short Writings from Bulawayo* anthologies and *Writing Now*. He's currently a doctoral student of literature specialising on the works of Dambudzo Marechera and Percy B. Shelley.

TOGARA MUZANENHAMO b.1975 in Lusaka, Zambia of Zimbabwean parents. He was brought up in Zimbabwe, studied in The Hague and Paris and became a journalist in Harare and worked for a script development company. His work has appeared in magazines in Europe, South Africa and Zimbabwe and his acclaimed collection, *The Spirit Brides*, was published in 2006 by Carcanet Press in the UK.

KUDZAI NDANGA works and lives in the United Kingdom. She loves writing poems and short stories, as well as reading good fiction.

DAVID NETTLEINGHAM b. 1984 in the UK. He is a doctoral student, researcher and teacher of sociology, founder of The Conversation Project for international poetry and co-editor of its English-language magazine. He is an editor and poet of the Dialecticist school of poetry and co-author of *Adage Adagio: Drafts I-X* (2009).

FISANI NKOMO b. 1971 in Mberengwa is a self-styled artist specializing in abstract and mixed-media painting. His works discuss social, political and socio-economic issues. He has exhibited at the Harare International Festival of the Arts (HIFA) and the National Gallery in Bulawayo among others. He's currently curetting an exhibition for the annual Intwasa Arts Festival koBulawayo.

KRISTINA RUNGANO b. 1963 in Harare and grew up near Kutama Mission. She attended Catholic-run boarding schools in Selous and Harare and teaches Business at Canterbury Christchurch University. She is Zimbabwe's first published female poet, and *A Storm is Brewing* (1984) is her first collection.

EMMANUEL SAIROSI grew up in the thriving ghetto of Nkulumane in Bulawayo, and describes poetry as "my closest companion." He is a recipient for the Southern African Scholar award to study for an MSc in International Development in Edinburgh, Scotland.

ZVISINEI SANDI b. 1973 in Mt Darwin in Zimbabwe. She is currently a Scholar Rescue Fellow at Stanford University's Centre on Democracy, Development and the Rule of Law. She previously taught at the Zimbabwe Open University and Masvingo State University. She is published in *Women Writing Zimbabwe* and *Creatures, Great & Small*.

EMMANUEL SIGAUKE teaches English at Cosumnes River College in Sacramento, California. He has published poetry in Zimbabwe, Ireland, Finland and the United States and has appeared in a wide variety of online journals. His publications include a poetry collection, *Forever Let me Go*, and a chapbook of short stories, *Mukoma's Return*.

BEAVEN TAPURETA b. 1975 in Chitungwiza. He is currently the Programme Officer at the Budding Writers Association of Zimbabwe head office, and also works as a freelance journalist. He has published short stories and poems in various local publications.

MICHAEL TSINGO b. 1983 in Bikita. He has an English degree from Midlands State University and a Masters in Journalism and Media Studies from the University of Witwatersrand in Johannesburg. He has extensive print and online media experience. He was a founding member of the MSU Writer's club, a once upon a time, campus get together creative writing forum.

PHILLIP ZHUWAO b. 1971 – d. 1994. He grew up on a commercial farm, north of Harare to immigrant parents of Mozambican and Zambian origin. He wrote in English but used neologisms, deliberate misspellings and slang from rural communities. His poetry collection, *Sunrise Poison*, will be published by Deep South, as well as two novellas.

Acknowledgements

For permission to publish and republish the poems in this anthology acknowledgement is made to the poets themselves and to the following copyright holders:

Abel Dzobo for his poems, 'City Blues' and 'The ZIFA Chairman'; Amanda Hammar for her poems, 'A man is dying for a piece of bread', 'Carla at the Miramar', 'Abandoned', 'Exiles' and 'Zimbabwe Lost' from Poetry International Website; Batsirai Chigama for her poems, 'Alien' and 'Poems in an Envelope'; Beaven Tapureta for his poems, 'Walking 'n Talking' and 'Worker's Day' from Munyori.com; Bettina Schmidt for Dambudzo Marechera's poems, 'For Bettina, A Tuesday Prologue', 'Shock: For Bettina', 'To Bettina with Angry Tenderness' from Poetry International Website; Chenjerai Hove for his poems, 'Nights with ghosts', 'Embraces in the rubble', 'Identity', 'Counting the nights', 'Tyrant', 'The Little Sister'; Christopher Mlalazi for his poems, 'A Soundless song', 'Where will they be on Xmas day?', 'The Worker's Flag', 'When will the serpent shed its skin?', 'They are coming'; Cosmas Mairosi for his poems, 'Amai Chido', 'Visions', 'Freedom', 'The Lord is my Shepherd', 'Still the same peasants' from Poetry International Website; Emmanuel Sairosi for his poem, 'Soon the Truth becomes apparent'; Emmanuel Sigauke for his poems, 'A House for Mother', 'The Village Motto', 'Bulawayo and Oslo', 'Gonera Bees' and 'Smitten with Art'; Ignatius Mabasa for his poems, 'Poetry' from *Illuminations*, 'Cavities', 'Concrete and Plastics', 'Defiance', 'Swings and See-saws' from Poetry International Website; Jennifer Armstrong for her poems and essay; John Eppel for his poems, 'Cewale' from *The Warwick Review*, 'An Awkward Gait' from *The European Messenger*; 'Pungwe [Matobo 1984]' from *Illuminations Kenya*, 'Sonnet with One Unstated Line' from *Short Writings From Bulawayo I*, 'Songbirds' and 'Hillside Road in August' from *Carapace*; Josephine Muganiwa for her poems, 'Nothing For Free' and 'Senior Pastor's Conference'; J. Tsitsi Mutiti for her poems, 'Lean Thinking', 'To give and not to count the cost' from Munyori.com; Julius Chingono for his poems; 'A Silhouette', 'As I Go', 'The Cult', 'Zhin Zhan' from Poetry International Website and 'My Uniform' from *ZimboJam*; Kristina Rungano for her poems, 'Londoners', 'Oh ye righteous man of Babylon', 'The sound of voices', 'Alien Somebody', 'A world without terror' from her manuscript *Harsh Noises & Soft Tunes*; Kudzai Ndanga for her poems, 'I am not my mother's daughter' and 'She is dead'; Masimba Biriwasha for his poems, 'Once Upon A Bloody Journey' and 'Wood'; Michael Tsingo for his poem 'Sovereignty'; Nhamo Mhiripiri for his poems, 'Interregnum: The short sleeve or long sleeve choice', 'When you meet my countrymen' and 'In African gulags'; NoViolet Bulawayo for her poems, 'Diaspora', 'Independence', 'Balance', 'Darfur' and 'Souvenir'; Robert Berold for Phillip Zhuwao's poems, '...and love wept', 'Mayakovsky', 'hush hush (harsh) my love', 'When thought remains', 'The jar of chrysanthemums' from *Sunrise Poison*; Rumbi Katedza for 'An Open Love Letter' and 'Last Dollar'; Ruzvidzo Mupfudza for his poems, 'Quest', 'A Binge at the Crossroads', 'Zimlife', 'Out of which the Mafia is hewn' and 'Songs of Bones'; Tinashe Muchuri for his poems, 'Fifteen Minutes Drive', 'Mother's Prayer', 'Running Away Men', 'Guest of Honour' and 'A Soldier's Confession'; Charles Mungoshi and Poetry International Zimbabwe for 'A Kind of Drought', 'Unemployed in the beer garden', 'Prayer', 'Nehanda' and 'The Man who ran way from pain' from www.poetryinternational.org; Tinashe Mushakavanhu for his poems, 'Tomorrow is Long Coming', 'In the house of Exile' from *Illuminations*, 'The Distorted Looking Glass', and 'Crossing the Divide' from *Exiled Ink!*; Togara Muzanenhamo for 'The Chronicles' and 'At Measure', from *Times Literary Supplement*; 'A Killing' and 'Amnesia', from *PN Review*; 'Buying Out the Dead' from *Radio Netherlands*; Zvisinei Sandi for her poems 'Is God A Woman' and 'Exhortation' from Munyori.com.

Every effort has been made to trace copyright holders, but in a few cases this has proved impossible. The publishers would be interested to hear from any copyright holders not here acknowledged.

Further acknowledgements go to Gus and Karly Henne for their help; Katie Blythe for her unwavering support; Christopher Hobday, Irene Staunton and Dominic Williams for their expert advice; Luigi Marchini, Federico Federici, Jeremy Clulow and Mary Smathers for their constant encouragement; and Lina Musasa for being a reassuring source of light.

Selected Bibliography

Bvuma, Thomas (n.d.) *Every Stone That Turns*. Mambo Press, Gweru
Chihota, Clement (1999) *Before the Next Song*. Mambo Press, Gweru
Chimsoro, Samuel (1978) *Smoke and Flames*. Mambo Press, Gweru
Chingono, Julius (1996) *Flag of Rags*. Quartz Press, Johannesburg
Chirikure, Chirikure (1998) *Hakurarwi*. Baobab, Harare
Eppel, John (1995) *Sonata for Matebeleland*. Snail Press, Harare
—— (2005) *Songs My Country Taught Me*. Weaver Press, Harare
—— (2007) *White Man Crawling*. 'amaBooks, Bulawayo
Hove, Chenjerai (1982) *Up in Arms*. ZPH, Harare
—— (1985) *Red Hills of Home*. Mambo Press, Gweru
—— (1998) *Rainbows in the Dust*. Baobab Books, Harare
—— (2003) *Blind Moon*. Weaver Press, Harare
Kadhani, Xavier (1976) *Quarantine Rhythms*. Mambo Press
Kadhani, Xavier and Zimunya, Musaemura (eds.) (1982) *And Now the Poets Speak*. Mambo Press, Gweru
Magadza, Chris (2006) *Father and other poems*. Poetry International Web <www.zimbabwepoetryinternational.org>
Mahoso, Tafataona (1989) *Footprints about the Bantustan*. Nehanda Publishers, Harare
Marcus, Deon (2005) *Sonatas*. 'amaBooks, Bulawayo
Marechera, Dambudzo (1978) *The House of Hunger*. Heinemann, London
—— (1992) *Cemetery of the Mind*. Baobab Books, Harare
Mhasvi, Roland (1992) *Flowers of Yesterday*. UZ, Harare
—— (1999) *Time of the Rupture*. Roland Mhasvi Publishers, Harare
Morris, Jane (2008) *Intwasa Poetry*. 'amaBooks, Bulawayo
Muchemwa, Kizito Z. (ed.) (1978) *Zimbabwean Poetry in English*. Mambo Press, Gweru
Mungoshi, Charles (1998) *The Milkman Doesn't Deliver Only Milk*. (2nd revised edition) Baobab Books, Harare
Mushakavanhu, Tinashe and Nettleingham, David (eds.) (2009) *State of*

the Nation: Contemporary Zimbabwean Poetry. The Conversation Paperpress, Kent

Muzanenhamo, Togara (2006) *The Spirit Brides*. Carcanet Press, Manchester

Ngara, Emmanuel (1992) *Songs from the Temple*. Mambo Press, Gweru

Nyamubaya, Freedom (1986) *On the Road Again*. ZPH, Harare

—— (1996) *Dusk of Dawn*. College Press, Harare

Nyathi, Albert (2008) *Echoes from Zimbabwe*. ZPH, Harare

Pongweni, A. (1982) *Songs that Won the Liberation War*. College Press, Harare

Rungano, Kristina (1984) *A Storm is Brewing*. ZPH, Harare

Sigauke, Emmanuel (2008) *Forever Let me Go*. PublishAmerica, Maryland

Style, Colin and O-Lan (1986) *The Mambo Book of Zimbabwean Verse in English*. Mambo Press, Gweru

Veit-Wild (1988) *Flora Patterns of Poetry in Zimbabwe*. Mambo Press, Gweru

Zhuwao, Phillip (forthcoming) *Sunrise Poison*. Deep South, Grahamstown

Zimunya, Musaemura (1985) *Country Dawns and City Lights*. Longman, Harare

—— (1982) *Kingfisher Jikinya and other poems*. Longman, Harare

—— (1982) *Thought Tracks and other poems*. Longman, Essex

—— (1993) *A Perfect Poise and other poems*. College Press, Harare